Margaret Ayer—

SIAM

OR

THE HISTORY OF THE THAIS

FROM 1569 A.D. TO 1824 A.D.

BY

RONALD BISHOP SMITH

with a frontispiece by

MARGARET AYER

Printed by
DECATUR PRESS, INC.
BETHESDA, MARYLAND
1967

TABLE OF CONTENTS

ACKNOWLEDGEMENTS

I wish to acknowledge a debt of gratitude to those benefactors who have assisted me in the creation of this volume. I would like to express my gratitude to His Excellency, Sukich Nimmanheminda, the Ambassador of Thailand to the United States, for reading my manuscript, and offering comments and suggestions for improvement of the present work. I would like to thank Miss Margaret Ayer for reading parts of my manuscript, for offering suggestions and for her many words of encouragement. And my mother, Florence Bishop Smith, for the correction of spelling and grammatical errors.

I also wish to thank Miss Christine Susan Mueller for her kind and generous assistance in translating (and assisting me to translate) numerous French passages without expense or charge to myself. Mrs. Cely Modesto Lawrence of the Brazilian Military Commission in Washington, D. C. for translating (as well as assisting me to translate) Portuguese and Spanish documents. And last, but not least, I wish to express my special thanks to my typist, Mrs. Ruth Boyd Tompkins, for her diligence in typing the final copy of my manuscript. I am indebted to Mrs. Tompkins not only for her thoroughness and proficiency as a typist but also for her care as a proofreader—in the former capacity for a small fee, and in the latter role without material reward.

RONALD BISHOP SMITH

PREFACE

Siam with the splendor of her ancient name, the glory of her past renown, and the deeds as well as the misdeeds of her sons, is the topic of my *Siam or the History of the Thais from 1569 A.D. to 1824 A.D.* In the present volume, as in my companion *Siam or the History of the Thais from Earliest Times to 1569 A.D.*, I have sought to introduce the varied actors of Thai history, each after his own manner, on a stage grounded firmly on historical fact: not one floated in the realms of conjecture or surmise. As we shall see the elucidation of early seventeenth century Siamese history, in particular, must be attempted with the greatest caution.

In the narration of the present history of Siam and the Thai people, I have utilized English, French, Portuguese and Spanish language sources, as well as Thai sources translated to English. Primary sources in the English language, upon which I have drawn, include the *Luang Prasoet* chronicle of Siamese history; the *Records of the Relations between Siam and Foreign Countries in the 17th Century*, containing the correspondence of merchants, statesmen, princes and kings; the works of Jeremias van Vliet, chief Dutch factor at Ayudhya (1636-41); the *Hmannan Yazawin Dawgyi* chronicle of Burmese history—a very valuable source for the description of the numerous Thai-Burmese wars; and the journal and correspondence of John Crawfurd for a relation of the customs, government and products of early nineteenth century Siam. Two important secondary sources for the study of Thai history are W. A. R. Wood's *A History of Siam* and Prince Chula's *Lords of Life*. Wood, in particular, has been my access to many Thai sources impenetrable to my ken because of my inability to read Thai. Other important secondary sources include the works of Hall, Giles, Anderson and Turpin.

The works of Maybon, Moura and Le Boulanger, in the French language, are respectively the most comprehensive histories for the study of Vietnam, Cambodia and Laos. Phayre and Harvey are useful authorities for the relation of Burmese history, and the works of Winstedt and Kennedy are recommended to the interested reader for the study of Malay history.

In the Appendix to this work, I have included four supplementary documents. Appendix I contains a description of the Burmese siege of Ayudhya in 1587; Appendix II a translation of the description of the first Spanish embassy to Siam in 1598; Appendix III a copy of the unequal Dutch treaty concluded between Siam and the Dutch East India Company in 1664; and Appendix IV a letter by Constantine Phaulkon to Father Tachard, relative to the French expedition to Siam in 1687. The letter has been translated from the Portuguese, as contained in the *Archivo Historico Portuguez*, Vol. I, Lisbon, 1903.

As brevity is the soul of wit, a consummation to be desired in a preface, I bring this Preface to a rapid conclusion by stating a Supplement has been placed at the end of the volume, containing translations (from the Portuguese)

8

of the descriptions of the first Portuguese embassies to Siam, as well as extracts (in old English) from the *Peregrination* of Mendez Pinto; may the discriminating reader have recourse to the Supplement as he pleases; and to the same reader, may I suggest he raise the curtain to the present production by turning this page.

RONALD BISHOP SMITH

BETHESDA, MARYLAND
NOVEMBER 7, 1966

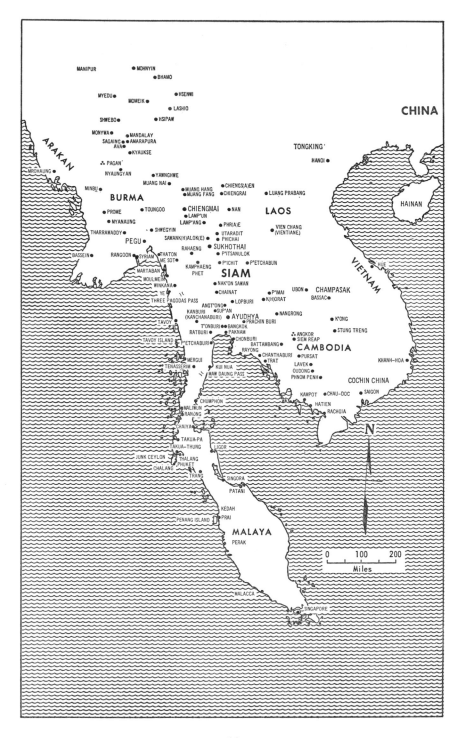

CHAPTER ONE

THE MIDDLE AYUDHYA PERIOD 1491 - 1629 — PART 4
UNTIL THE DEATH OF KING NARESUEN IN 1605

I. THE BURMESE DOMINION IN SIAM 1569 - 84

Victory, the votary of so many Siamese martial enterprises in former years, had seemingly forsaken the Thai banners to march with the legions of the kings of Burma, Tabinshwehti and Bayinnaung. The Kingdom of Siam in the year 1569 had temporarily reached the nadir. Defeated and coerced by the Burmese, disgraced by the treachery of P'ya Chakri, beset by hostile nations, the prospects for the recovery of Thai independence were bleak indeed. To make a bad situation worse the Cambodians, in the traditional manner, attacked the Siamese at the moment of Ayudhyan degradation. Amid the downfall of kingdoms, the din and clash of arms and the extinction of dynasties a new leader arose, a valiant prince, who eventually delivered his people from their bondage.

Prince Naresuen, later King Naresuen (1590-1605), was the elder son of King Maha T'ammaraja I. Prince Naresuen was taken captive by Bayinnaung (and forced by the Burmese monarch to accompany his return to Burma) in 1564 following the Burmese invasion of Siam. A sister of the prince married Bayinnaung who, in 1571, allowed Prince Naresuen to return to his country, perhaps out of deference to the wishes of his new bride. Naresuen was sixteen when he returned to his native land. The resource and bravery which the young prince displayed in repulsing the invading Cambodians at this time made him the hope of his countrymen. Their faith in him was not misplaced.[1]

King Bayinnaung, before returning to Burma, demolished the defenses of the Siamese capital. Burmese officials were placed in high position residing in Ayudhya as well as other cities in the kingdom. Burmese laws and institutions were introduced as well as a new system of dating known as the Chulasakarat (Chulasakaraj) Era. The Chulasakarat or Little Era commences the dating of years from 638 A.D. It remained in use in Siam until 1887, replacing the Mahasakarat Era introduced in southern India in 78 A.D. The introduction of the Laws of Manu * apparently belongs to the period 1569-84.[2] The influence of Burmese culture was, therefore, not inconsiderable in Siam during the fifteen year period of Burman domination.

In 1570 King Boromoraja (1566-76) of Cambodia, in search of loot and plunder, invaded the stricken Kingdom of Ayudhya. He expected an easy seizure of the now defenseless capital, but instead met with a vigorous defense and was forced to retire with heavy losses. The Cambodian king probably indemnified himself for whatever losses he sustained by carrying away Thai settlers, as prisoners, to enrich his own country with the fruits of their industry. The Cambodian attack of 1570 afforded the Siamese the opportunity of rebuilding the defenses of Ayudhya without provoking the distrust of their Burmese overlord. As a consequence new walls were erected, and new canals were constructed to ensure defense against the Cambodians. Cannon were also purchased from the Portuguese.[3]

---

* A code of behavior of Hindu derivation.

11

King Bayinnaung, not replete with his conquests in Thailand, undertook the invasion of the Kingdom of Laos (Lang Chang) in 1574. Both his vassals, King Maha T'ammaraja I and Prince Naresuen, were compelled to accompany the Burman potentate on the Lao expedition. Prince Ekat'otsarot, the brother of Naresuen and later king of Ayudhya (1605-20), assumed the responsibilities of regent in Ayudhya during the absence of his father and brother. Apparently the services of Prince Ekat'otsarot were not long in demand because his brother, Naresuen, was taken ill with smallpox before he reached Laos, and as a consequence, both he and the king of Siam were granted permission to return home—the Burmese proceeding to Laos without Siamese assistance.[4] With or without Siamese help the affairs of the great Burman monarch prospered. In 1575 he placed his own candidate, Oupahat (1575-80), on the Laotian throne. King Bayinnaung had reduced one more Asian kingdom to a state of vassalage. Not until 1592 did the Laotians finally repudiate the suzerainty which bound them to Burma.[5]

War, in Siam, was renewed with Cambodia in 1575.

> "In [C.E.] 937 [1575 A.D.], the year of the pig, Phraya Lavek
> [king of Cambodia] came with war boats to Ayuddhya. On
> Saturday the 10th of the first waxing moon the people of
> Lavek [Cambodia] established themselves at Phaneng Xong;
> in the battle which ensued the Cambodians were unable to
> offer effective resistance, and their army returned." [6]

Three years later Siam again suffered from a Cambodian invasion. Although the Cambodians were repulsed, large numbers of prisoners were captured by the invaders.[7] The tribulation of the common people in Thailand at this time must have been great, although Siamese history does not tell us much about their sufferings.

> "We can, however, easily guess that at this period they had
> reached the lowest possible degree of misery and want. Num-
> berless men had been killed in the wars with Burma, and
> thousands more had been swept away into slavery in Burma
> and Cambodia. The few who remained were barely able, we
> may suppose, to plant the rice crop from year to year; yet all
> had to work like slaves in order to raise the tribute payable
> to the King of Burma." [8]

Naresuen, who was known as the Black Prince,* displayed his military prowess and personal courage in helping to stay the Cambodian invasion of 1578. Following the invasion, P'ya Chin Chantu, a Cambodian nobleman who acted as a spy for his country, made his escape from Ayudhya presumably after the discovery of his nefarious activity. He was pursued by Princes Naresuen and Ekat'otsarot. Apparently P'ya Chin Chantu escaped from his pursuers, as the *Luang Prasoet* states he returned to Lavek (as Cambodia is sometimes called in the Thai chronicle), although an:

> ". . . action ensued, in which Prince Naresuen astonished all
> beholders by his reckless disregard of danger. From that time

---

* Naresuen was called the Black Prince from the darker color of his skin as compared to his brother, Ekat'otsarot, who was known as the White Prince.

onwards he began to be looked upon, both in Siam and in Burma, as the one man likely to undertake the difficult task of freeing his country from Burmese dominion." [9]

In the same year (1579) the Princess Maha Tewi, the regent of Chiengmai since 1565, died. King Bayinnaung appointed his son, Tharawadi Min, as a vassal prince of Chiengmai. The prince assumed the title of Nohrata Zaw.[10]

In C.E. 942 (1580 A.D.) King Maha T'ammaraja I demolished the walls of Ayudhya, and erected new ones.[11] In C.E. 943 (1581 A.D.) a serious rebellion broke out in the eastern part of the Ayudhyan kingdom. The rebel, Yana Prajien, defeated and killed the general sent to subdue him. The royal troops went over to the side of the rebels. According to the *Luang Prasoet* "Yana Prajien studied occult science." The rebel leader, however, whatever his theoretical proficiency in the science, was deficient in practical execution, subsequently meeting his death in attacking Lopburi. His followers were dispersed.[12]

The king of Cambodia, Satt'a or Chettha I (1576-94), raised an army in C.E. 943 (1581 A.D.), invaded the Kingdom of Ayudhya, and captured the city of Bejrapuri (Phet Buri?). In the following year the Cambodians invaded eastern Siam, and carried off many people.[13]

II. THE SIAMESE WAR OF INDEPENDENCE 1584-1605

King Bayinnaung died in 1581 at the age of sixty-six. The great conqueror was succeeded on the Burmese throne by his son, Nanda Bayin (1581-99).[14] Burmese rule in the Kingdom of Ayudhya did not long outlive King Bayinnaung.
"Bayinnaung had sown the wind; his son reaped the whirlwind. Not that Nanda Bayin was lacking in either ability or determination, but sooner or later the reaction against his father's extravagance and megalomania must come." [15]

When King Nanda Bayin ascended the Burmese throne the numerous Burmese vassals were called upon to pay homage to the new king. The Siamese king was unable to attend, but his son, Prince Naresuen, represented his father. While the Black Prince was in Burma an insurrection against Burmese rule erupted at Muang Kum in the Shan country. King Nanda Bayin ordered Prince Naresuen with his Siamese troops, and two Burman princes with their forces, to suppress the rebellion. The Thai prince captured the city after both Burmese princes had tried and failed. The success of the Black Prince seemingly aroused the jealousy of the Burmese, and his relations with the Burmese deteriorated. He returned to Siam in 1582; according to some accounts pursued by the Burmese to the frontier. Whatever the manner of his departure, Prince Naresuen saw the weakness of the Burmese empire in the less able hands of the successor of the great Bayinnaung. He resolved to throw off all ties with Burma at the first suitable opportunity.

The Burmese, no doubt suspicious of the loyalty of their Siamese vassals, made preparations for war against Ayudhya. During the year 1583 the road leading to Kamphaeng Phet, at that time included within the territory of the tributary principality of Chiengmai, was improved, and supplies were collected at the city. Undoubtedly the intention of Nanda Bayin was to invade Siam at the end of 1583. Difficulties, however, in the form of an insurrection by the Burmese vassal, the king of Ava, delayed the attack on the Siamese kingdom.[16]

King Nanda Bayin, perhaps a little shamefacedly, requested the services of his vassal, Prince Naresuen.* Surprisingly, the Black Prince came with his forces. According to Wood, King Nanda Bayin planned to have the prince assassinated. Two noblemen from Pegu were sent to accompany the Siamese prince to Burma. They were instructed to murder the prince while on the march. Prince Naresuen met the emissaries of his destruction at a place called Muang K'reng.

> "After meeting him the intended assassins were touched by his youth and his gallant bearing; their consciences revolted against their infamous task, and they divulged the plot to the Prince." [17]

The Black Prince, having been forewarned of the murderous disposition of King Nanda Bayin, renounced on behalf of his father, all allegiance of the Kingdom of Ayudhya to Burma. The Siamese declaration of independence was proclaimed at Muang K'reng in May of 1584. There followed many years of desperate combat in what we shall call the Siamese War of Independence (1584-1605). Although the Siamese were hard pressed during the early stages of the mortal conflict, nevertheless they had so far recovered from the hard blows inflicted by Tabinshwehti and Bayinnaung, they were definitely able to take the offensive against their Burman antagonists in the later years of the war. [18]

As long as his forces were armed and ready for war Prince Naresuen decided to give his ex-suzerain a few hard blows for the nonce. Finding the Mon border population favorably disposed, the Black Prince marched on Hanthawadi (Pegu). The Burmese forces at Pegu were commanded by Minkyi-zwa, the crown prince of Burma. Prince Naresuen laid siege to the city with a large force, described by the *Hmannan Yazawin Dawgyi* as consisting of three hundred elephants, three thousand horse and sixty thousand men. The crown prince of Burma prepared to make a vigorous defense, but before the Black Prince could launch an assault against the city he learned that King Nanda Bayin had defeated the king of Ava and was moving on Pegu. Naresuen, less than confident about meeting the Burmese, and their victorious king, decided to raise the siege of Pegu. The Black Prince returned to Siam by way of Mottama (Martaban), collecting a large number of Thai prisoners who had been captured during previous Burmese invasions of Siam. [19]

The king of Burma, angered at the defection of his vassal, dispatched an army led by Crown Prince Minkyi-zwa to force the submission of Naresuen. The Burmese were defeated by the prince. Wood states the defeat occurred on the banks of the Sittaung (Sittang). [20] The *Hmannan Yazawin Dawgyi* relates that a Burmese force of about one hundred and twenty thousand men encamped at a place called Sotkali north of Ayudhya. Prince Naresuen, who the Burmese chronicle wrongly entitles king, made a sortie from the capital, defeating the Burmese and forcing their retirement (we unfortunately are not told to what place). [21] Hall states the Burmese were defeated in the Menam Valley, a statement, which if not telling all we wish to know, at least has the merit of not being incompatible with the battle-location given in the *Hmannan Yazawin*

---

* King Maha T'ammaraja I reigned until his death in 1590, although he seems to have left most of the governing functions of his office to Prince Naresuen.

14

Dawgyi.[22] The location of the place of battle will perhaps never be known. In any case the battle, wherever it was fought, brought the Siamese their first major victory gained against the Burmese for many years.

King Nanda Bayin was not easily discouraged by the defeat of his forces. His son was recalled, and a new expedition was sent to recapture Shan prisoners who had escaped from Burma and taken up abode at P'itsanulok. The invasion, perhaps, was not a serious attempt to subjugate Thailand, but may have been more in the nature of a reconnaissance to test the defenses of Siam. Whatever the underlying purpose of the expedition the result was uniformly unfortunate for the Burmese. The Burmese advanced as far as Kamphaeng Phet from which point, however, they were driven back across the frontier by the Siamese. The governors of Sawankhaloke and P'ijai (Phichai) conceived the Burmese army to be a mighty instrument of war greater than the facts of the situation warranted. Placing their fears above loyalty to their own sovereign, they declared for the Burmese cause, fortifying themselves in Sawankhaloke. Prince Naresuen dealt with the miscreants in summary fashion, storming Sawankhaloke, and executing the disloyal governors.

King Nanda Bayin showed himself in his distress more determined than ever. In order to bend the Siamese to his will, preparations on a greater scale were necessary. An army of thirty thousand men, led by the prince of Bassein, advanced on Ayudhya by way of the Three Pagodas Pass in December of 1584. The Burmese war plan provided for the union of the prince of Bassein, with the prince of Chiengmai who marched, supposedly, with one hundred thousand men.

The Siamese had made preparations commensurate with the threat which confronted them. Three separate armies were raised; one under P'ya Chakri,* another army placed under the command of the governor of Sukhothai and a third army led by two anonymous princes of Siam. The total forces which the Kingdom of Ayudhya had at its disposal may have numbered fifty thousand men. Thus if our figures are correct the Siamese were at a considerable numerical disadvantage. However, they reacted to the situation by adopting a novel strategy. A large portion of the northern population of the Kingdom of Siam was removed to the precincts of the capital city. A scorched earth policy was adopted as the rice crop was collected or destroyed. Other supplies were no doubt removed or destroyed at will. Thus the forces allotted to the Chiengmai contingent, if they marched by the direct route from Chiengmai to Ayudhya, must have experienced want and privation on the march, important elements, no doubt, in the subsequent Burmese defeat.

The Burmese, instead of uniting their two armies at some point for a simultaneous advance on Ayudhya, committed their forces one after another thus enabling Prince Naresuen to defeat each in detail. The army of the prince of Bassein arrived at Sup'an before the Chiengmai troops could support him. The Siamese defeated the prince of Bassein after several engagements forcing the enemy across the border (between Siam and Burma). In February 1585, some two weeks after the final defeat of the Burman army in the south, the prince of

---

* A different person than the traitor of ill-famed repute described in my *Siam or the History of the Thais from Earliest Times to 1569 A.D.*, p. 96, 97.

Chiengmai belatedly marched into Siam encamping at Jainat (Chainat). His forces, as we have indicated, were probably suffering from the effects of privation. Nevertheless, the forces commanded by the prince of Chiengmai were apparently larger than those of Naresuen, since the latter could not defeat the Burmese in a pitched battle, but was obliged to resort to guerrilla tactics. The prince of Chiengmai, in subsequent skirmishes, suffered numerous losses eventually retiring on Kamphaeng Phet.[23]

Prince Chula in his book the *Lords of Life* portrays the gallant behavior of the Thai national hero in the following terms.

> "By the lightning movements of his mobile columns, consisting mostly of cavalry, Naresuan in several successful skirmishes much weakened both of the two Burmese forces before they could form a junction. By then his own personal daring and deeds of bravery had become a legend, and it helped to inspire his troops to emulate him and know no fear. In fact King Maha Tammaraja had once to rebuke his son for being too intrepid. This was when he heard that Naresuan had led the assault of a Burmese camp by climbing the wooden ramparts with the blunt side of a sabre held in his mouth." [24]

Rather than accept responsibility for the disaster which had befallen his forces, King Nanda Bayin laid the blame for failure at the door of his brother, the vassal prince of Chiengmai, Tharawadi Min (Nohrata Zaw), who had not executed his part of the war plan with sufficient promptitude. The king of Burma peremptorily ordered the prince of Chiengmai to advance on Nakhon Sawan, and to make preparations for a further campaign in the Ayudhya kingdom. The crown prince of Burma with fifty thousand men took up position at Kamphaeng Phet to facilitate the preparations. Once again we must relate how the Burmese dispositions were thrown into confusion by the supple strategy of the Black Prince. The Burmese were defeated in several preliminary engagements after Tharawadi Min had established his camp at Sraket not far from Angt'ong. In April 1586 the Burmese forces were ambushed by the Siamese who employed the old ruse of a feigned retreat so effectively employed against them on previous occasions. In the rout which followed the Burmese lost ten thousand men, one hundred and twenty elephants, as well as four hundred boats. The prince of Chiengmai escaped from the tumult only by leaving his personal property behind to fall into the eager hands of the Siamese.* Thus two years and four invasions after the Siamese declaration of independence King Nanda Bayin had not yet realized his object: the suppression of the independence of the Thai Kingdom of Siam.

We have recorded four successive military triumphs which redound to the credit of the Black Prince. However, it behooves us as impartial students of Thai history to relate an incident showing how Prince Naresuen let his anger get the best of his judgment; a fact which had diplomatic repercussions of consequence in the mortal struggle of the Kingdom of Ayudhya against her implacable Burman adversary.

---

* No mention of this defeat is to be found in the *Hmannan Yazawin Dawgyi*.

16

About the year 1585 King Satt'a (1576-94) of Cambodia, contrary to the usual canons of Thai-Cambodian relations, concluded an alliance with the king of Siam. During the fourth invasion of Siam (1586) King Satt'a sent an army, led by Prince Srisup'anma, to co-operate with Prince Naresuen in repelling the attack of the prince of Chiengmai. It remains unclear what produced the sudden spate of co-operation between the ancient rivals especially as in years past Thai struggles in the west often induced the Cambodians to attack from the east. The alliance was apparently the first time the two kingdoms had ever co-operated in a joint enterprise. Unfortunately a grotesque incident marred the friendship which had developed between the two countries.[25]

> "The Black Prince considered that Prince Srisup'anma treated him with discourtesy during the return journey to Ayut'ia, and retaliated by causing the severed heads of some . . . prisoners to be impaled close to the boat of the Cambodian Prince. The latter complained to his brother, on his return to Cambodia, of the treatment which he had received. King Satt'a was greatly offended, and determined to abandon the alliance with Siam as soon as a good opportunity should arise."[26]

If Prince Naresuen had suppressed his anger his country might have been spared a war with Cambodia at the time of the decisive siege of Ayudhya in 1587. The Siamese could then have concentrated their entire energies on defeating the main foe. Instead the Siamese kingdom was obliged to fight a war on two fronts, to the misery and detriment of her people. Nevertheless, as we shall see, Prince Naresuen (King Naresuen after 1590) was equal to waging a war on two fronts. Indeed after 1592 he was able to take the offensive against his enemies.

King Nanda Bayin, notwithstanding repeated failures, or the sore punishment meted to his armed forces; notwithstanding the bloodshed, misery and dislocation of life in Burma and Thailand was not yet ready to recognize the independence of his recalcitrant neighbor. His efforts to crush the independence of the Thais (Thai means free) called forth greater efforts straining the resources of his kingdom to the full.

Unmindful of the previous defeat of Crown Prince Minkyi-zwa, King Nanda Bayin placed his son once again at the head of an expedition (April 1586). The invading army consisted of nineteen brigades totaling, perhaps, one hundred and twenty thousand men including no doubt contingents from Chiengmai. The Burmese army marched to a place called Lagun (Burmese designation). On hearing of the renewal of the invasions Prince Naresuen marched from Ayudhya with an army of fifteen brigades. A skirmish, presumably near Lagun, tested the skills of five Burmese and four Siamese brigades with results unfavorable to the latter. The Siamese thereupon retired to a well-fortified position at Sotkali north of Ayudhya. The Burmese failed to storm the position although they made two assaults. Threatened with the exhaustion of their provisions the Burmese, as a last measure, feigned a retreat hoping to induce the Siamese to leave their strong position. Prince Naresuen, perhaps, not unaware of the enemy's intention, followed the Burmese with his forces seeking to inflict a decisive defeat. When the Burmese learned that the men of Ayudhya were following in force they halted and formed in three divisions. The left and right divisions consisted of six brigades each. The center division was brought into line by the crown prince of Burma who had seven brigades under his immediate command.

Prince Naresuen, coming upon the Burman battle positions, perceived in an instant the weakness of the Burmese deployment. The right wing of the enemy was posted in a strong natural position while the left wing was exposed.* The Black Prince concentrated his forces for an attack on the left wing. His attack was immediately successful. The Burmese in the exposed position were completely routed. Prince Naresuen now rolled up the left flank forcing the center division under Crown Prince Minkyi-zwa to give way. The Burmese on the right, however, were in a strong position, and they withstood the Siamese assaults. Although able to maintain its position, the Burman right division was unable to repair the damage inflicted upon the left and center divisions. The remnants of the Burmese army were collected, returning to Hanthawadi (Pegu) in August of 1586.** [27]

The victory of Prince Naresuen is more remarkable when we consider that he had defeated the prince of Chiengmai in April 1586 with forces probably numerically inferior to those of the enemy. The troops of the Black Prince were undoubtedly fatigued after their exertions; the succession of Burmese invasions had impoverished his country and worst of all no respite was in sight. The king of Burma with untold art seems to have possessed the power to conjure new armies from the blue. No matter how fiercely he was smitten, he sprang forth again, usually with more imposing strength. He never relaxed the pressure against his adversary for an instant. Thailand it seems was in a death-grip with a legendary hydra, a creature losing appendages, lopped off by the strong sword of the Black Prince, only to be replaced by a remarkable power of regeneration. Many Thais during the violent times in which they lived must have despaired of seeing their land free and at peace with the world. But for the moment they had no alternative but to continue the war, longing for better days, or bow their heads submissively to the yoke of King Nanda Bayin. However painful the Siamese chose to resist as best they could.

Once again the sound of marching soldiery could be heard in Burma. King Nanda Bayin mobilized a vast army which, according to the *Hmannan Yazawin Dawgyi*, was:

> ". . . composed of twenty-four brigades, containing 3,200 elephants, 12,000 horse, and 252,000 men, and [Nanda Bayin] left Hanthawadi [Pegu] on Sunday the 9th of waxing Tazaungmon 948 (November A.D. 1586), leaving his son the Maha Upayaza [Crown Prince Minkyi-zwa] in charge of the capital." [28]

The Siamese made preparations for resistance adopting expedients indicating the urgency of the moment.

> "The whole available population was gathered together at Ayut'ia and all the crops, ripe and unripe, were either har-

---

* I have made the assumption that the Burmese line of battle was facing southward, and that the Siamese were marching north.

** The *Luang Prasoet* does not mention the Burmese Invasion of April-August 1586.

vested or destroyed. Small bands of men, under leaders experienced in guerrilla tactics, were collected for the purpose of harassing the Burmese whenever a chance offered. No attempt was made to hold the surrounding country, except to the south, where it was . . . of paramount importance to maintain communication with the sea." [29]

Three Burmese armies marched on Ayudhya arriving simultaneously in January of 1587.[30] King Nanda Bayin launched several assaults against the fortified Siamese positions, but was repulsed owing to the adept manner in which the Ayudhyans employed their guns (artillery). The Burmese king then prepared for a long siege, but notwithstanding the vastness of the Burman army he was not able to effectively block the exits of the city, largely because of the width of the rivers and streams. Well-conducted sorties, led by the Black Prince, further reduced the effectiveness of the siege.* Indeed the very vastness of the Burmese army now proved its undoing. For miles around, the countryside had been swept bare of provisions. The army of King Nanda Bayin soon began to feel the effects of hunger. Sickness and privation depleted the ranks of the army, and King Nanda Bayin, fearing the dissolution of his army once the rainy season commenced, raised the siege of Ayudhya in May of 1587. The Black Prince harassed the retreating foe. He, however, received a check by the Burmese rear guard under the king of Toungoo at Indaw (Royal Lake). Perhaps the Ayudhyans might have pursued the Burmese with more success if the situation in the east had been less threatening.[31]

The reader will recall that Prince Naresuen had not acted toward Prince Srisup'anma, the brother of the Cambodian king, with proper circumspection during the expedition which defeated the prince of Chiengmai in April 1586. King Satt'a of Cambodia upon hearing of the Burmese invasion of Thailand, decided to avenge his brother's insult (whether real or imaginary) as well as, no doubt, sweep in as much plunder as possible. The Cambodians captured Prachim (Prachin Buri?), but shortly after the siege of Ayudhya, Prince Naresuen drove the Cambodians from their recent conquest as well as from Thailand. The Black Prince advanced into Cambodia as far as Lavek, capturing Battambang and Pursat, before he was obliged to withdraw because of lack of supplies.[32] The Siamese took with them many horses, elephants and prisoners—the usual loot in a Cambodian raid.[33]

King Maha T'ammaraja I died in July of 1590.

"He was aged seventy-five and had reigned for twenty-one years. In his youth active and patriotic, he became in middle age a traitor to his country, and ascended the throne when Siam had sunk into a state of degradation for which he was himself largely responsible. As King, he appears to have been a nonentity, wisely leaving the conduct of affairs to his sons. He lived long enough to see Siam once more free; but he must often have reflected with sorrow that it was his sons, and not himself, who severed the chains which he had helped to forge." [34]

---

* See Appendix I for a description of the siege in the quaint language of the *Luang Prasoet.*

Naresuen was now king in name as well as in fact. He was thirty-five years old when he ascended the throne of Ayudhya. His first act was to appoint his brother, Prince Ekat'otsarot, for whom he had great affection, to the office of Maha Uparat or vice-king. Prince Ekat'otsarot did not govern from P'itsanulok, in accordance with ancient custom, because of unsettled conditions in the northern countryside. Instead he remained at Ayudhya.[35]

The Kingdom of Ayudhya observed three years of uneasy peace during the period 1587-90. The kingdom by no means had recovered from the effects of war. Rice was selling at famine prices, and adding to the hardships of the people, nature visited the kingdom with two recorded earthquakes.[36]

King Nanda Bayin, however, was not a man to let other people's misfortunes thwart his ambition. Once again we find him preparing for a renewal of the war. Sometime during 1590 a council was held in Burma to discuss how a Shan rebellion at Mogaung could be suppressed. The advice was tendered that an intimate connection existed between the so far successful rebellion at Ayudhya and the unrest in the Shan country, and that unless the Siamese were forced to submit there was the likelihood of a general rebellion throughout the Shan districts of Burma. A decision was therefore reached to act against the Kingdom of Siam at once. An expedition; described by the *Hmannan Yazawin Dawgyi* as consisting of twenty-four brigades, one thousand elephants, ten thousand horse and two hundred thousand men; was commanded by Crown Prince Minkyi-zwa for the invasion of Siam. The army left Hanthawadi (Pegu) in November 1590 [37] marching into Siam by the Three Pagodas past Kanburi (Kanchanaburi). The Burmese intended to reach Ayudhya before the Siamese could organize an effective defense, but the Burman army itself was surprised by King Naresuen not far from the frontier.[38]

> "King Bra Narit [Naresuen] of Yodaya [Ayudhya] went out and opposed the Burmese at Lagun. He placed the weak portion of his army on the road to Lagun to act as a decoy while he himself with sixty nobles and sixty of his best elephants lay in ambush in the forest close by. The Maha Upayaza [Crown Prince Minkyi-zwa] and his commanders, seeing the Siamese forces, advanced in battle order and fought bravely. . . . The Siamese forces which acted as a decoy retreated followed by the unsuspecting Burmese, when at the right moment, Bra Narit [Naresuen] came out from the ambuscade and fought the enemy fiercely. The Burmese were put to utter rout, with a very heavy loss in killed and wounded. The governors of Pagan and Pathein (Bassein) fell into the hands of the Siamese. It was with difficulty that Maha Upayaza gathered in his scattered forces. He returned to Hanthawadi [Pegu] in haste and arrived in the month of Tagu (April 1591).[39]

Siamese military strategy had come a long way since that dark day in 1548 when King Tabinshwehti employed a similar ruse against the Siamese with equal effect.

The king of Siam now took the offensive against the Burmese albeit abortively. He ordered a force of fifty thousand men including the governor of

20

P'itsanulok, as well as three other governors, to advance into Burma (1591). They were however assaulted, by the Burmese governor of Mottama (Martaban), in a fortified position at Winyaw (Winkana?). The Siamese were defeated, and retreated to their own country.[40]

We now come to the last of the great Burmese invasions of Thailand during the Siamese War of Independence. King Nanda Bayin decided to make a final effort to subdue the Kingdom of Siam.[41] He was, perhaps, buoyed by the recent success of his forces. In December 1592 the Burmese monarch assembled his followers, and severely rebuked them. He declared that his sons, ministers and noblemen all enjoyed the royal bounty, but did not render proportionate service to his person and kingdom. He compared unfavorably his liegemen with those who served the zealous and self-sacrificing king of Ayudhya. He exhorted his followers to make one more supreme effort against the enemy.

An army, divided into twenty-six brigades, including two hundred and forty thousand men as stated in the *Hmannan Yazawin Dawgyi*, was mobilized for service in Siam. Included in the immense host, soon to tread the soil of Thailand, were fifteen hundred elephants and twenty thousand horse, a force if properly led and supplied should have been sufficient to trample underfoot all opposition. The vassal kings of Prome, Toungoo and Chiengmai each led contingents. The entire force, commanded by the inept Crown Prince Minkyi-zwa, marched from Hanthawadi (Pegu) in December 1592.[42] Apparently one part of the army advanced by way of the Three Pagodas, and the other part by the Me Sot route.[43]

King Naresuen, late in 1592, was preparing to attack Cambodia when he received news of the Burmese invasion.[44] The redoubtable Thai king prepared to meet the Burman attack. Unfortunately Burmese and Thai accounts differ on many of the particulars of the invasion. The Burmese *Hmannan Yazawin Dawgyi* states that the Burmese army arrived at Ayudhya in February 1593 and battle was joined outside of the city. The crown prince of Burma, so the chronicle relates, was killed by a gunshot while riding on his elephant in the midst of battle. In the Burmese version the Burman army gained the victory, but returned to Burma without effecting anything of note.[45]

Wood, whose account is largely substantiated by the *Luang Prasoet*, relates a somewhat different story. When King Naresuen was apprised of the Burmese invasion, including the descent of the two Burmese armies upon his kingdom, he determined to attack whichever force arrived first. The crown prince of Burma advanced to Trap'angkru, northeast of Sup'an. The second Burman army never got beyond Melamao. Thus once again the Burmese made the fatal mistake of dividing their forces neglecting to ensure a rapid reunion at the decisive point of attack. Nevertheless, the army of the crown prince alone was greatly superior in numbers to the army which King Naresuen commanded. The Thai king when he realized the disproportionate size of the contending forces scrapped his offensive plans, and awaited the inevitable attack from a strong position at Nong Sa Rai thirty miles east of the Burmese army.

P'ya Sri Sai Narong, with a small detachment, received orders from King Naresuen to reconnoitre the Burman position, but not to attack the Burmese. P'ya Sri Sai Narong, contrary to orders, became heavily engaged with the enemy. He received a message from King Naresuen, who could hear the sputter of gunfire in the distance and, perhaps, the booming of the Burmese artillery, to break off the engagement. P'ya Sri Sai Narong was in no position to disobey this order. His force was no longer a coherent body, and it bolted in great disorder toward the Siamese lines. This otherwise unfortunate incident had an unsettling effect on the Burmese who unwittingly approached the main Siamese army, which was fully prepared to meet a now disordered Burmese foe, hot in pursuit of a broken Thai detachment. The tactics which the Siamese employed at the Battle of Lagun ca. 1591 (i.e. drawing the Burmese upon the main Siamese army) were again employed. In the present battle, however, they were the result of the fortuitous meeting of opposing Thai and Burmese forces contrary to the orders of King Naresuen.[46] Thus chance was a dominating element in the decisive drama now unfolding, the stakes of which were no less than the freedom or bondage of the Kingdom of Siam.

King Naresuen and his brother, Prince Ekat'otsarot, were both mounted on their elephants as the Burman army drew near.

> "The noise and excitement of the Burmese onrush so maddened these two animals that they flung themselves furiously forward through the front ranks of the Burmese army; almost before they knew what had happened, the King and the Prince found themselves, accompanied only by their immediate attendants, in the midst of the Burmese host. As soon as the elephants could be stopped, and the dust had subsided, the King saw, to his surprise, the Crown Prince of Burma (whom he had known well in former days) close by him, also mounted on an elephant. He at once called out: "Brother Prince, leave the shelter of that tree. Come out and fight with me, for the honour of our names and the wonder of future ages!"
>
> The Burmese Prince had but to say a word and the Siamese monarch and his brother would have been overwhelmed and either killed or captured. Though a poor General, he was, however, a brave man. Scorning to refuse such a challenge, he drove his elephant forward, and the two Princes joined in single combat. The Prince dealt a fierce blow with his sword at the King's head. The latter bent in time to avoid the blow, but the leather cap which he was wearing was cut through. The elephants broke away, but were brought forward for a second charge. This time the Burmese Prince received a wound in the shoulder and fell dead from his elephant.
>
> Thus perished the unfortunate Prince Min Chit Swa [Minkyi-zwa]. He was forced by his father to undertake a task for which he had no capacity. He was, we learn, most unwilling to command this last expedition . . . he died bravely, fighting against the most redoubtable warrior ever produced in Siam." [47]

Prince Ekat'otsarot overcame the prince of Zaparo whom he slew in single combat. King Naresuen, as Wood relates, received a wound in the hand, but he and a handful of his followers, fighting desperately in the Burmese midst, were rescued from further danger by the timely arrival of Siamese troops forcing their way through the Burmese ranks. The Burman army, demoralized by the death of the crown prince and sorely pommeled by the Ayudhyan assaults, retired toward the western frontier. The Siamese did not press the pursuit for fear of a Burmese attack on their rear by the army encamped at Melamao. The fear of attack from that quarter proved groundless, as the Melamao army was recalled when King Nanda Bayin received the news of the death of his son.[48]

King Nanda Bayin, after numerous invasions of the Kingdom of Siam (we have recorded eight), had reached the end of his tether. His kingdom, exhausted by years of warfare and exorbitant demands for military service, was on the verge of revolt. Thousands of Mon subjects abandoned their own country to escape the exactions of the Burmese king[49] while famine stalked the delta of the Irrawaddy—the richest part of the Burmese Empire. Rebellion soon convulsed the once powerful Burman state,[50] and as we shall see King Naresuen took advantage of the confusion prevailing in Burma to aggrandize his own kingdom. The year 1593, therefore, marks the turning point in the Siamese War of Independence (1584-1605). At the Battle of Nong Sa Rai the ominous Burmese threat to the independence of Siam, which like a dark, heavily laden thundercloud, had occasionally showered its bolts of destruction on the Thais, received a salutary check. The Burmese were not to pose a serious threat to the independence of the Kingdom of Siam for more than one hundred and fifty years.

King Naresuen, following his return to Ayudhya, expressed dissatisfaction with the conduct displayed by some of his military commanders in the recent campaign. The king accused them of gross negligence, because they had failed to follow the king through the Burmese ranks. An inquiry was held concerning the matter. The king recommended the death penalty, but the intercession of the Buddhist clergy mollified the anger of the great Thai king. He agreed to pardon the offenders on one condition only, namely that the offenders agree to capture the territories of Tavoy and Tenasserim which had been severed from the crown of Ayudhya, in 1568, by King Bayinnaung of Burma.

Two armies, each containing fifty thousand men, commanded by two suspect leaders (determined to rewin the favor of the king) advanced on Tavoy and Tenasserim in 1593. P'ya Chakri besieged Tenasserim which he captured after a fifteen day siege. P'ya P'rak'lang was equally successful, capturing Tavoy after a sharp skirmish and a twenty day siege. Meanwhile the Burmese, not unmindful of the commercial value of both places, had assembled a fleet of two hundred ships for the transportation of an army to Tenasserim. The fleet from Burma fell in with a fleet of one hundred and fifty Siamese ships, assembled by P'ya Chakri to aid his brother general, who he erroneously believed needed assistance in the prosecution of the siege of Tavoy. P'ya P'rak'lang, in equal ignorance of the outcome of the siege at Tenasserim, despatched a fleet of one hundred ships to assist at that siege. While the Burmese were engaged in mortal strife with the fleet of P'ya Chakri, the ships of P'ya P'rak'lang appeared at the scene of battle. The Burmese, now outnumbered by the Ayudhyan fleet, were defeated. The Burmese fleet reached the mouth of the Irrawaddy as best it could.* [51]

---

* The sea battle was presumably fought between Tenasserim and Tavoy, perhaps off Tavoy Island in the Andaman Sea.

Thus by the concurrence of an accidental meeting at sea, compounded by a double Thai ignorance, an important naval advantage was gained by the Siamese. Lady fortune which had deserted the Thai cause during the invasions of King Bayinnaung now gave the Siamese an unexpected, almost undeserved victory. Nevertheless, if we have no reason to applaud the preconceived strategy by which victory was obtained, P'ya Chakri and P'ya P'rak'lang to their credit, showed a willingness to co-operate with one another—a disposition not universally accorded to all military leaders, or Thai generals, past and present.

The willingness of the two Thai leaders to pool their resources was also an essential element in a decisive victory gained by the Ayudhyans on land, north of Tavoy. The Siamese had learned from captured Burmese naval prisoners that a strong Burmese army was advancing on Tavoy. P'ya Chakri, after the recent, but victorious, dispatch of his fleet, marched northward to Tavoy with thirty thousand troops. He arrived to find his fellow general in possession of the city, but threatened with the loss of his new conquest by the approach of the Burman army. Men were landed from the victorious Thai ships, and a combined force of ninety thousand men awaited the Burmese foe at a position near Tavoy. The Burmese sustained a disastrous defeat. The Thai occupation of Tavoy and Tenasserim was thus assured by the Siamese victory, and the two generals as well as subordinate commanders so recently ostracized by King Naresuen, were once again re-established in the good graces of the king of Ayudhya.

Tavoy and Tenasserim formed lucrative additions to the Kingdom of Siam. The provinces were centers of a large foreign trade—evidenced by the ability of the Siamese to commandeer two hundred and fifty ships on short notice. An extensive export trade in sappanwood, elephants and spices of many varieties was cleared through the provinces for Asian and world markets. Thus King Naresuen could expect increased revenues as well as an expansion in his capacity to wage future wars.[52]

With the ebbing of the Burmese threat to Siamese independence, King Naresuen was briefly able to take in hand the reconstruction of the devastated parts of his kingdom. Efforts were made to repopulate northern Thailand. In 1594 numerous prisoners were captured in King Naresuen's Cambodian campaign (yet to be described), and resettled in different parts of the kingdom. Many of the unfortunate Thais captured by King Satt'a in previous incursions were released and resettled in the northern provinces. The king, no doubt, made further efforts to revitalize the economy of his kingdom. The population of the kingdom as a whole had suffered a grievous decline as a result of the repeated invasions during the second half of the sixteenth century. The population of Siam, perhaps, did not reach the pre-1548 level until the present century.[53]

King Naresuen, however, showed less disposition to cultivate the arts of peace than to engage in the martial rigors of a soldier's life. The reader will recall that King Naresuen was preparing to attack Cambodia, late in 1592, when his energies were diverted in another direction by the Burmese onset. King Naresuen now prepared to deal King Satt'a a vigorous blow. Preparations were completed by May 1593, and an army, perhaps 50,000-100,000 men, marched into Cambodia. The expedition was accompanied by a large fleet of boats.

The Cambodians were unable to withstand the might of King Naresuen, inured to war by a succession of military triumphs. Battambang and Pursat fell to the great Thai warrior king with little or no resistance. At a place called Boribun, Prince Srisup'anma, took up position with thirty thousand men, but soon hesitated to match arms with King Naresuen. The prince fled to Lavek— at this date the capital of Cambodia. Boribun was an easy conquest. King Naresuen advancing on Lavek was joined by Siamese forces from the north which had captured Siemrap (Siem Reap) and Bassac and other cities north of the Tonle Sap. The Cambodians stoutly defended their capital, but in July 1594 the city was taken by assault. The losses on both sides were heavy.[54] King Satt'a fled from his capital, eventually retiring to Laos where he died, in exile, in 1596. Prince Srisup'anma was taken prisoner, but the often repeated story that King Naresuen washed his feet in the blood of the Cambodian king is apocryphal. Apparently the Cambodians, for a few years at least, recognized a tenuous tie of suzerainty to the Ayudhyan king.[55] Hall states that King Naresuen did not attempt the annexation of the kingdom, but sought to inflict a paralyzing blow so that he could better prosecute the war against the main enemy.[56]

In 1594 King Naresuen renewed the war with Burma. The Mon population, wearied by the repressive measures of King Nanda Bayin, was ripe for rebellion. The Mon governor of Moulmein raised the flag of revolt. He requested military assistance from King Naresuen against the Burmese governor of Martaban who was attempting to repress the insurrection. The king of Siam with an army of thirty thousand men captured Martaban, and prepared to meet the king of Toungoo who had been ordered to drive the Siamese out of Burma.[57] The *Hmannan Yazawin Dawgyi* relates that the king of Toungoo commanded a force of eighty thousand men, four hundred elephants and four thousand horse. His army totaling eight brigades was defeated by a combined force of Mons and Thais. The king of Toungoo was obliged to retreat,[58] according to Wood as far north as Thaton.[59] The Burmese defeat apparently occurred in either November or December 1594.[60] As a consequence of the successful encounter with the Burmese, a large part of the old Kingdom of Pegu recognized Siamese suzerainty.[61]

The edifice of the Burmese Empire, wrought by the hammering blows of King Bayinnaung, was crumbling in the dust. Already in 1592 King Nokeo Koumane (1591-96) of Laos formally proclaimed the independence of his country from Burma thus undoing the work of King Bayinnaung in that direction.[62] In 1595 King Nokeo Koumane quarreled with the prince of Chiengmai (Tharawadi Min). Tharawadi Min sought the assistance of Nanda Bayin, his suzerain, but the king of Burma was fully preoccupied with unsettled affairs closer to home. Tharawadi Min, threatened with the loss of his throne, applied to King Naresuen for help. The king of Ayudhya, not unnaturally sought to augment his influence over the onetime hereditary enemy of Ayudhya.[63] In 1598 King Naresuen sent reinforcements which drove the Laotians out of Chiengmai. Tharawadi Min, in return for the services received, placed Chiengmai under the suzerainty of the king of Ayudhya.[64]

"In the light of subsequent events, it appears that this was a mistaken policy. King Naresuen could have easily annexed the whole of the Chiengmai dominions to Siam. Had he done

25

so, the dawn of the seventeenth century would have seen him ruling over a strong and united Tai Empire. He missed a great opportunity, and as a result the northern and southern Tai drifted apart, and were never truly united together until about three hundred [two hundred?*] years later." [65]

In 1598 Don Tello de Aguirre, a Spaniard, arrived in Siam from Manila, and succeeded in concluding a Treaty of Amity and Commerce between the kings of Spain and Siam. The treaty, only the second between a European power and the Kingdom of Ayudhya,[66] was a precursor to greatly increased contacts with Europe established in the early years of the seventeenth century.

In Burma proper all semblance of unity disappeared after 1594. The prince or vassal king of Prome, incensed because he was not elevated to the office of crown prince, attacked the prince of Toungoo, believing he was responsible for the slight cast upon him.[67] Confusion spread throughout the kingdom. King Nanda Bayin, the supreme king, was powerless to deal with the internecine strife engendered by his turbulent relations who governed Prome, Ava and Toungoo. The Arakanese, who in the past had felt the Burman flail, captured Syriam in 1599, and joined forces with the army of the prince of Toungoo besieging Pegu at that time.[68] King Naresuen himself incapable of duplicity, fell victim to the wiles of the king of Toungoo who along with the Arakanese invited the Thai king to participate in the invasion of Burma apparently making great promises. The scheming king of Toungoo had second thoughts about the utility of Siamese assistance, indeed he probably feared it. The king of Toungoo, therefore, sent agents to Martaban and to other parts of Pegu under the suzerainty of Siam to foment rebellion. By the summer of 1599 the newly acquired Peguan provinces were in a state of revolt against their Siamese overlord. Order was restored, but when King Naresuen arrived at Hanthawadi (Pegu), in October 1599, he found a smouldering ruin. The allies of the Thai king had deserted him, and indignation swelled within his breast. King Naresuen decided to revenge himself against the perfidy of the king of Toungoo by invading his realm, and inflicting the condign punishment which Naresuen believed he deserved. Toungoo was besieged by King Naresuen, but to no avail. The Siamese suffered greatly from sickness and starvation, and in May of 1600 the siege was raised. The miscarriage of Thai operations at the siege of Toungoo was the first military failure, of consequence, experienced by Naresuen. Nevertheless, despite the defeat, the field of war in the last stages of the Siamese War of Independence (1584-1605) was shifting to Burmese soil, to the relief of the Thai people long oppressed by the deluge of Burman warriors trampling their life's work underfoot.[69] King Nanda Bayin, whose mailed coils all but crushed the breath of life of the Kingdom of Siam, despairing of maintaining order in his own kingdom, placed himself under the protection of the king of Toungoo. The king of Burma was ignominiously hustled off to Toungoo where shortly after he was poisoned.[70] So passed the most obstinate if least successful potentate ever to wage war against the Kingdom of Siam—a pathetic end to the son and successor of the great conquering Bayinnaung.

---

* Chiengmai was finally annexed to the Kingdom of Siam in 1775.

King Naresuen, on the return journey from the unsuccessful expedition to Burma, was asked to settle a dispute between the prince of Chiengmai, his vassal, and P'ya Ram Dejo, who acted as a resident (or adviser) in Chiengmai in the interests of the king of Ayudhya. Prince Ekat'otsarot, the White Prince and brother of King Naresuen, was commissioned by the king to resolve a dispute concerning the respective rank of Tharawadi Min and P'ya Ram Dejo—the latter claiming a rank at least equal to the former. The dispute was settled to the satisfaction of the prince of Chiengmai.[71]

> "This incident well illustrates the honourable character of King Naresuen. By encouraging P'ya Ram Dejo, or even by letting matters take their own course, a position would have been brought about which would have rendered it an easy matter to annex the whole dominions of Chiengmai to Siam. Tharawadi Min had, however, placed himself under the protection of Siam, and had since acted as a loyal vassal. King Naresuen therefore supported him, even though it was strongly against his own interest to do so." [72]

King Naresuen, as Phayre tells us, retreated by way of Martaban. Before returning to Ayudhya he made the Mon, Binnya (P'ya) Dala, governor (or vassal king) of Martaban; and an individual called Byathabaik, was created tributary king of Tavoy.[73]

The war with Burma, erupting with volcanic force in times past, was now gradually dying a natural death. Five years of uneasy peace between the two rival kingdoms followed the ill-fated Siamese expedition of 1599-1600. At peace with Burma, King Naresuen once again allowed himself to become involved in Cambodian affairs. We have already mentioned how King Naresuen defeated the Cambodians in 1594, and have indicated that the Cambodians were reduced to a tributary status if only temporarily. Following the expulsion of King Satt'a (1576-94) from his kingdom by the Siamese, several rulers feebly swayed the royal sceptre in the ancient land of the Khmers.[74] Portuguese and Spanish adventurers intervened in the civil wars of troubled Cambodia adding to the confusion. The Siamese tie of suzerainty had, as a consequence of the confusion, lapsed, and King Naresuen, therefore, was eager to proffer his assistance when the queen mother, supported by the Kingdom of Cambodia as a whole, petitioned for the return of Prince Srisup'anma, held captive by King Naresuen since the war of 1593-94. Prince Srisup'anma was released, and mounted the throne of Cambodia taking the style Srey Sauryopor (1603?-18) or Soriyopur. He remained a loyal vassal of Siam.[75] Wood states that six thousand Siamese troops were needed to help the new king ascend his throne, a fact concerning which Cambodian history is apparently silent.[76]

King Naresuen, during the five-year lull in the war with Burma found time to intervene in the turbulent affairs of the Shan states, successfully detaching some of them from their allegiance to Burma replacing Siam in her stead. Three Shan states: Hsenwi, Muang Nai and Muang Hang came under Siamese protection. The king of Ava (Sihasu T'ammaraja; or Nyaungyan Prince as Hall describes him) who claimed the supreme kingship in Burma, was determined to regain the allegiance of the lost Shan principalities. When the prince of Muang Nai found himself threatened by the Burmese, he invoked the aid of his suzerain, the king of Siam. King Naresuen, not realizing he was girding himself for the last campaign, marched northward to rescue his distressed vassal. The great warrior king received large reinforcements at Chiengmai on the way, but alas all was for nought. On arriving at Muang Hang the valiant king was stricken with a carbuncle on the cheek. Divining that now he must in his turn pay the debt which nature exacts from her creatures—king, peasant or beast alike—King Naresuen sent for his brother at Muang Fang (about thirty miles away), and prepared for death. In May 1605 King Naresuen, with his beloved brother at his side, passed away at the early age of fifty. [77]

Ekat'otsarot, now the king of Siam, decided to abandon the expedition on which his brother had embarked. The remains of the former king were cremated at Ayudhya, and the vassal states of Hsenwi, Muang Nai and Muang Hang once again passed under Burmese control.[78]

Finally it remains to draw a picture, as best we can, of the character and accomplishments as well as failings of King Naresuen, sometimes referred to as Naresuen the Great. Without question he was a great leader of men, a valiant man of arms and a skilled practitioner of the military art. His skill, his bravery and perseverance, were major factors in the re-establishment of the independence of his country—an accomplishment which alone establishes his reputation. King Naresuen, nevertheless, seems to have had some of the defects which great warriors are prone. The *Hmannan Yazawin Dawgyi* implies that he drove his men in battle so that they feared him more than death.[79] The continuation of King Naresuen's Burmese incursions after 1593, and his intrusions into Cambodia, suggest an excessive interest in war at a time when his country was no longer threatened with the loss of her independence. The Kingdom of Siam needed peace to rebind her wounds not aggrandizement at the expense of her neighbors, notwithstanding the important conquests made in 1593 and afterward. A disposition to cruelty is evidenced by the *Luang Prasoet* which states that one hundred Peguan prisoners, who had angered the king, were burnt alive.[80] Perhaps the now absolute nature of the Siamese monarchy made such displays of arbitrariness inevitable. Perhaps the age in which King Naresuen lived was more cruel than others. But to whatever we ascribe the defects of the great Thai monarch, whether to circumstance, time or solely to personal volition, his name holds an honored place in the history of Siam as the Liberator of the Thais.

BIBLIOGRAPHY

1. Chula, H.R.H. Prince. *Lords of Life*, Taplinger Publishing Co., Inc., New York, 1960.
2. "Events in Ayuddhya from Chulasakaraj 686-966," *Journal of the Siam Society*, Vol. VI, Part 3, Bangkok, 1909. English translation by Frankfurter, O.
3. Ghosh, Manomohan. *A History of Cambodia*, J. K. Gupta, Saigon, 1960.
4. Hall, D. G. E. *A History of South-East Asia*, MacMillan & Co., Ltd., London, and St. Martin's Press, New York, 1961.
5. "Intercourse between Burma and Siam, as recorded in Hmannan Yazawindawgyi," *Journal of the Siam Society*, Vol. V, Part 1, Bangkok, 1959.
6. Phayre, Sir Arthur P. *History of Burma*, Trubner & Co., London, 1883.
7. Wood, W. A. R. *A History of Siam*, The Siam Barnakich Press, Bangkok, 1933.

FOOTNOTES

1. Hall, 218, 219. Hall states that Pra Naret (Naresuen) was taken prisoner to Burma after Maha T'ammaraja became vassal king of Ayudhya, i.e. 1569; See Hall, 218. Wood, who I have followed in this matter, states the prince was taken to Burma in 1564; See Wood, 128. Perhaps the subservience of Maha T'ammaraja to Burmese interests can be partly explained by fear for the safety of his son.
2. Wood, 126, 127.
3. Ibid., 127, 128.
4. Ibid., 128, 129.
5. Hall, 217, 218.
6. "Events in Ayuddhya, etc.," 14.
7. Wood, 129.
8. Ibid., 130.
9. "Events in Ayuddhya, etc.," 14, and Wood, 129.
10. Wood, 129, 130.
11. "Events in Ayuddhya, etc.," 14.
12. "Events in Ayuddhya, etc.," 14, and Wood, 130. Wood assigns the rebellion to the year 1580.
13. "Events in Ayuddhya, etc.," 15.
14. Wood, 130.
15. Hall, 218.
16. Wood, 131, 132.
17. Ibid., 132.
18. Ibid.
19. "Intercourse, etc.," 126, and Wood, 132.
20. Wood, 132, 133. Wood states that the musket used by Prince Naresuen (Pra Naret) in the Siamese victory was for many years part of the regalia of Siam, and was known as the "Musket of the Battle of the Sittaung River." From this fact Wood gives credence to the Siamese account of the location of the battle as opposed to the Burmese account; See Wood, 133.
21. "Intercourse, etc.," 126, 127.
22. Hall, 219.
23. Wood, 132-34.
24. Prince Chula, 45, 46.
25. Wood, 133-35.
26. Ibid., 135, 136.
27. "Intercourse, etc.," 127-29.
28. Ibid., 130. Wood states the crown prince accompanied the expedition as commander of one of the army divisions. The army was divided into three parts. The two other commanders were the king of Burma himself and his brother, the prince of Taungu (Toungoo); See Wood, 136. The *Luang Prasoet* mentions a certain Mahauparaj (perhaps the crown prince of Burma) as fighting against the Siamese at the siege of Ayudhya; See "Events in Ayuddhya, etc.," 16.
29. Wood, 136.
30. Ibid.
31. "Intercourse, etc.," 130-32.

32. Wood, 137.
33. "Events in Ayuddhya, etc.," 17.
34. Wood, 137, 138.
35. Ibid., 139.
36. "Events in Ayuddhya, etc.," 17.
37. "Intercourse, etc.," 135.
38. Wood, 139, 140.
39. "Intercourse, etc.," 135, 136.
40. Ibid., 136.
41. Wood, 140.
42. "Intercourse, etc.," 137.
43. Wood, 140.
44. Ibid., 140, 141.
45. "Intercourse, etc.," 137-39.
46. Wood, 141-43.
47. Ibid., 142, 143.
48. Ibid., 143.
49. "Intercourse, etc.," 139.
50. Phayre, 122.
51. Wood, 144, 145.
52. Ibid., 144-46. No mention is made of the Siamese capture of Tavoy and Tenasserim in either of the translated versions of the *Luang Prasoet* or *Hmannan Yazawin Dawgyi* which I have used. Wood apparently has relied on one of the versions of the *P'ongsawadan* chronicle of Siamese history.
53. Wood, 146, 148.
54. Ibid., 146, 147.
55. Ibid., 147, 148; Consult also the history of Antonio de Morga, 1559-1636.
56. Hall, 222.
57. Wood, 148, 149.
58. "Intercourse, etc.," 140.
59. Wood, 149.
60. "Intercourse, etc.," 140.
61. Wood, 149. Hall states that King Naresuen threatened Pegu, but was forced to retreat by the prince of Toungoo; See Hall, 222.
62. Hall, 218.
63. Ibid., 222.
64. Wood, 151.
65. Ibid.
66. Ibid., 149, 150; Consult also my Appendix II.
67. Wood, 150; Consult Hall, Phayre and G. E. Harvey as background to Burmese history.
68. Hall, 222, 223.
69. Wood, 152, 153.
70. Ibid., 152-54.
71. Ibid., 153, 154.
72. Ibid., 154.
73. Phayre, 123.
74. Wood, 155.

75. Ghosh, 238.
76. Wood, 155.
77. Ibid., 155, 156.
78. Ibid., 156, 157.
79. "Intercourse, etc.," 137.
80. "Events in Ayuddhya, etc.," 18.

CHAPTER TWO

THE MIDDLE AYUDHYA PERIOD 1491 - 1629 — PART 5
Until the Death of King At'ityawong in 1629

I. EKAT'OTSAROT 1605-20

The Kingdom of Portugal, throughout the sixteenth century, continued to monopolize European contacts with Siam. Suddenly, in the seventeenth century, there blossomed a great expansion of intercourse between European, as well as Japanese merchant enterprises, and the once relatively isolated Kingdom of Siam. Siam commenced to enter the calculations of monarchs, their ministers and the courts of Europe and Japan. Thai affairs were observed, and later discussed and weighed in the balance, as the great trading nations of the world competed for markets and advantages at the court of Ayudhya. The Siamese found themselves alternately cuddled and coerced, the object of attention or abuse as foreign rulers, merchants and merchant-adventurers with ever mounting strife sought the wealth of the east. Dutch, Japanese and later French influences were prominent at Ayudhya. Indeed our knowledge of Siamese history, in the seventeenth century, is in large part derived from the correspondence of merchants trading at Ayudhya and other Thai cities. The availability of new sources is especially significant in the absence of trustworthy Siamese documents since the reliable *Luang Prasoet* does not chronicle events after C.E. 966 (1605 A.D.). Indeed, one of the most surprising features of the period 1605-29 is the prevailing confusion among authorities concerning the reignal years of the various kings, even at this comparatively recent date. It rests incumbent upon us to try to resolve the disputes as best we can.

The Japanese were the first of the new foreigners to settle in Siam. The islanders, in many instances, were recent converts to Christianity immigrating to the Kingdom of Ayudhya to escape persecution under the intolerant policy of the Shoguns. The victories of King Naresuen over the Burmese, and the establishment of more tranquil conditions made possible the peaceful flow of trade, attracting Japanese merchants, as well as adventurers, to the Siamese kingdom. The Japanese, commanded by their headman Yamada, were granted their own settlement by King Ekat'otsarot. The Thai king enrolled a large force of Japanese immigrants in his bodyguard with Yamada as leader. King Ekat'otsarot also exchanged complimentary missions with the Shogun of Japan.[1]

In far off Europe two events of the year 1594 eventually had far-reaching effects on Siamese relations with the rest of the world. In 1594 Philip II, king of Spain, and since 1580 also king of Portugal, closed the port of Lisbon to Dutch and English shipping as a consequence of the wars fought between the Iberian king on one hand and the Dutch and English on the other. The decree of Philip II merely had the effect of stimulating Dutch and English enterprise, eventually breaking the Portuguese monopoly of the eastern trade with the occident. The Dutch, who were the first to organize the assault on the Portuguese position, were dissatisfied with their situation as middlemen in the distribution of trade between Lisbon and the rest of Europe. They now commenced to make the voyage direct to the east to tap the commerce of the orient at its source.[2] The Dutch commercial effort was facilitated by the formation of the *Compagnie van Verre* (Company for trade afar), in 1594, by Dutch merchants of Amsterdam, an event worthy of note in Siamese history. The first trade fleet of the company sailed from Texel in 1595. Other fleets followed as the Dutch assault on the Portuguese monopoly began in earnest. The fifth fleet of the company sailed for the Indies with six ships under the command of Jacob van Neck. After various misadventures two ships, the *Amsterdam* and *Gouda*, arrived at Patani in the autumn of 1601 thus inaugurating relations between Holland and the Siamese tributary state. Despite opposition from the Portuguese, Japanese and Chinese merchants, Admiral van Neck concluded a treaty with the queen of Patani providing facilities for the pepper trade, and allowing the Dutch to build a factory. Admiral van Neck remained at Patani until August 1602, overseeing the construction of the Dutch factory placed in charge of Daniel van der Leck of Rotterdam.[3]

By the year 1602 numerous Dutch trading concerns had been formed for trade with the east. The launching of the rival English East India Company on December 31, 1600 (O.S.) spurred the Dutch to unite competing interests to preserve their position in the face of English competition. In March 1602 the United East India Company or V.O.C. (*Vereenigde Oostindische Compagnie*) was granted a monopoly of Dutch trade between the Cape of Good Hope and the Magellan Straits for a period of twenty-one years. The new organization sought to co-ordinate the activities of the Dutch merchants in the east. The Dutch company, under the new order, had a clear financial advantage over their English counterpart, beginning operations with about ten times the capital of the English company.[4]

The Hollanders made their first appearance at the court of Siam in 1604, during the reign of King Naresuen. Admiral Wybrand van Warwyck, Dutch envoy extraordinary, was well received by the king of Siam in spite of Portuguese and also Spanish intrigues against his visit. Van Warwyck's visit opened direct intercourse between the Siamese kingdom and the Dutch republic.[5]

The Dutch opened a factory at Ayudhya in 1608. The following year the first recorded Siamese embassy to arrive in Europe was received by Maurice of Nassau (1584-1625), the Dutch stadtholder.[6] The ostensible purpose of the embassy was to establish friendly relations. King Ekat'otsarot, however, instructed the members of the mission "to study the technique of building foundries and to obtain handicraftsmen." [7] From the Dutch viewpoint the Kingdom of Ayudhya offered a valuable market for the sale of cloth and other manufactured products, and for the purchase of hides and sappanwood for export to Japan and for rice exported to Java. In due course the growing Dutch trade with Siam necessitated the opening of trading establishments at Ligor, Singora (valuable for the tin trade) and other places.[8]

The Portuguese, who for almost one hundred years had been masters of Siamese trade with the western world, were determined to maintain their paramountcy at Ayudhya. In 1606, the first Portuguese Jesuit, Father Balthazar de Sequeira, visited Siam. Father Balthazar was a man of many virtues including prudence; experienced in missionary work in the orient, although advanced in years. He left St. Thomas (in India), and reached Tenasserim, and then traveled across the Peninsula to the capital: ' "partly by goodly Rivers, partly over cragged

and rough Hills and Forrests, stored with Rhinocerots, Elephants, and Tigers . . .
unto Odia [Ayudhya]." ' [9] Apparently the ministrations of Father Balthazar did
not gain many converts or dispose the Siamese more favorably toward the Portuguese. He was, however, able to attend to the spiritual needs of the Portuguese
community from what was, perhaps, the only Christian church in Thailand.[10]

The Portuguese contemplated military as well as spiritual means to make the
nations of the east amenable to their wishes. In the following letter the king
of Portugal * lays bare his tiger's tooth:

EXTRACT OF A LETTER FROM THE KING OF PORTUGAL TO HIS VICEROY IN INDIA

Dated Lisbon, 4th January 1608 (N.S.)
26th December 1607 (O.S.)

". . . the rebels [the Dutch] maintain much communication
with the King of Siam, and took his Ambassadors to Holland,
with the aim of securing a league and friendship with him,
assuming to found a fortress in one of the ports of his Kingdom. . . . And that this King of Siam is one of the greatest
of those parts both in power of men as in wealth, and if the
rebels introduce the exercise of war and artillery, as it is
understood they are endeavouring to do, it will be an irrep-
arable evil; And that by making a Fortress in Martavan, so
close to the said King of Siam, it appears he will not dare to
afford the Dutch the position they pretend to in his Kingdom. . . ." [11]

Although the Portuguese viewed seriously the Dutch encroachment on what was
once their exclusive preserve, they apparently never executed the threat to build
a fortress at Martaban. At any rate Binnya (P'ya) Dala, appointed governor
(or vassal king) of Martaban by King Naresuen ca. 1600, was still commanding
at that city as late as 1613.[12] Mention is also made of an embassy sent by the
viceroy of Goa to King Ekat'otsarot at this time imploring him to expel the
Dutch from his kingdom. The Portuguese were running a gauntlet of argu-
mentative expedients; including the persuasions of cross, cudgel and diplomacy
in an effort to prevent the king of Siam from entering into closer contact with
the Dutch. King Ekat'otsarot, in fact, only granted the Dutch greater facilities
to engage in commercial enterprise including the ownership of Mergui Island at
the mouth of the Tenasserim River.[13]

King Ekat'otsarot gained a reputation among foreigners for being a covetous
man, because he devoted much of his time to the reorganization of the finances
of his kingdom. The king also imposed a new tax on his subjects. The tax,
apparently levied on shops and markets, was probably one of the earliest taxes
levied in cash.[14]

"The earliest form of taxation was the "tribute," sent by provinces or feudatory states to the King. Such tribute might be
merely nominal—such, for instance, as the gold and silver
trees sent by some of the Malay Rajas even during the present
century—or actual, such as supplies of timber, rice or fruits.

* Philip III (1598-1621) of Spain, as well as Portugal.

In later years it became usual to make cash payments, not only
in commutation of these "tributes" but also in commutation
of personal services due by individuals to the Government." [15]

The Kingdom of Siam and Western Europe were advancing from a feudal to a
money economy.

We are now brought face to face with one of the significant problems of
Thai history. The year 1610 has traditionally been given as the date of the death
of King Ekat'otsarot.[16] However, notwithstanding the consensus among many
authorities, we shall try to show that King Ekat'otsarot, the White King, retained
the kingship of Siam until 1620. In a letter dated the 4th October 1620 (N.S.),
written at Singora by the Dutchman Jan van Hasell to Jan Coen at Batavia
(Jakarta), the writer speaks of the illness of the old king and the incapacity of
the young one to rule.[17] Now the old king can be no other than King Ekat'otsarot
who as Wood states was born about 1558,[18] and therefore was about sixty-two
years old when the before-mentioned letter was written. King Ekat'otsarot was
succeeded either by Sri Saowaphak (according to the *P'ongsawadan*) or by
Songt'am (as Wood holds). Both Sri Saowaphak and Songt'am (or Int'araja II)
were sons of King Ekat'otsarot.[19] It seems improbable that either son of King
Ekat'otsarot was as yet forty years of age, and therefore the epithet "old" applies
to King Ekat'otsarot, himself sixty-two years old. It is yet possible to show that
King Ekat'otsarot not only ruled until 1620, but that he died the same year.
The following extract of an anonymous report submitted to the English East
India Company confirms the supposition:[20]

THE DESCRIPTION OF SIAM

"Siam many years ago, it seem, hath been a famous Kingdom,
bearing rule over others, ever being in good credit with the
King of China. . . . The King of Siam, Raja Api (or the Fire
King) [King Naresuen] died in 1605, whom his brother
(called the White King) did succeed. He died also 1620,
and his second son inherits, who now lives, and upon whom
many Kings do make wars and do hope to put him out of
his Throne." [21]

Supported by the foregoing evidence, we conclude that the reignal years of King
Ekat'otsarot were 1605-20, and not 1605-10 as previously supposed.*

Some years after the commencement of King Ekat'otsarot's reign, a tragic,
because unnecessary, death deprived the king of his eldest son, Prince Sut'at. The
king bears a heavy measure of responsibility for the death, indeed by most
accounts he caused the execution of his son whom he believed plotting to gain
the throne.[22] According to Siamese history:

"In the third year of the reign the King appointed his eldest
son, Prince Suthat, to be Maha Uparaj or Crown Prince. Four
months later the Crown Prince sought an audience with his

---

* I have subsequently learned, shortly before this book went to press, that Peter
Floris, who traveled in eastern waters before his death in 1615, assigns the
death date of Ekat'otsarot to the year 1610, thus kicking part of the starch
out of my certitude, yet the reasoning remains, and 1620 remains the more
probable date of death on the strength of the argument presented.

father. . . . The King turned on his son and enquired whether it was his intention to rebel. The Crown Prince was so overcome by fear of his father's suspicion that he retired from the royal presence, returned to his own palace, and in the evening committed suicide by taking poison." [23]

Since King Ekat'otsarot's reign commences in 1605, and if the death of Prince Sut'at occurred about the third year of his reign, his demise belongs to the year 1607-08. Giles declares that King Ekat'otsarot believed his son to be in communication with foreigners (later described as Laotians) for purposes of rebellion ca. 1611 or 1612,[24] therefore, by his account at least, precluding a death as early as 1608. Foreigners, we learn, were frequent visitors to the capital of Siam.

"During the reign of King Ekat'otsarot many states were the vassals of Siam. Ayudhya, the great and glorious city, attracted people from all over the world. . . . Envoys with their retinues from foreign and vassal states were frequently in Ayudhya." [25]

The death of Prince Sut'at is assignable to the period 1608-12. To ascribe the exact year of his decease, however, would be a mark of presumption with the meagre evidence at hand.

Wood suggests that King Ekat'otsarot may have been mentally afflicted at this period. We need not, however, try to draw the line between mental disease and outright vice, neither explanation being improbable. Wood further states that King Ekat'otsarot died beset by remorse for the death of his son.[26]

About the year 1611 the Japanese in Siam exploded in revolt. According to Wood's account (of the confused events of the time) the execution of the Japanese adherent, P'ra Nai Wai, sparked the rebellion. Two hundred and eighty Japanese "forced their way into the King's private apartments, and compelled him to sign in his own blood an ignominious treaty accepting all the conditions which they saw fit to impose." [27] Wood assigns the revolt to the reign of King Songt'am. We deny that Songt'am was king of Siam at this time. If therefore we accept the circumstances of the revolt, as described by Wood, the circumstances must be ascribed to the reign of King Ekat'otsarot. Wood further states the conditions which the Japanese sought to impose. They:

". . . included the surrender of four prominent officials who had rendered themselves obnoxious to the Japanese, the grant of various residential and commercial privileges, and the delivery to the insurgents of some of the chief priests as security for the performance of the King's promises. The unfortunate officials, on being surrendered to the Japanese, were immediately massacred." [28]

The Japanese sacked Ayudhya, and then proceeded to P'etchaburi (Phet Buri), erected fortifications, and prepared for the inevitable Siamese vengeance.[29] The Japanese did not have long to wait as the aroused Siamese fell on P'etchaburi and drove the insurgents out of their stronghold.[30]

The Laotians, aware of the internecine ebullitions bubbling at cross-currents in the Thai kingdom, sought to intervene in Siam to their own advantage. The following extract, of a letter written by the contemporary Dutchman, Cornelius

36

van Nyenrode (apparently chief Dutch factor at Ayudhya), provides an intimate glimpse of the Laotian invasion:

EXTRACT OF THE LETTER FROM CORNELIUS VAN NYENRODE & C. AT JUDEA (AYUDHYA) TO H. JANSSEN AT PATANI
Dated Judea, 3rd May 1612 (N.S.)
24th April 1612 (O.S.)

"Moreover during the revolt of the Japanese a great lord of this place named Chao Fa Tana[31] had gone over to the Langesander [Laotians] and told the King that the King of this place had been killed by the Japanese and that they were ruling the country, also that most of the people had fled. The King of the Lanchang [Laotians], one of the mightiest kings except this one here, has ordered his people to march hither and try to chase the Japanese and take the kingdom in their own possession. While marching against this town he found little resistance, so he has kept his camp about one day's journey hence during already 4 months, at a place called Lemvo [Lavo], and often sent Ambassadors (saying) that he had come to assist the king to turn the Japanese out of his country. However, His Majesty did not believe it, as the Lanchang people had brought many wives and children with them; and the latter made their intention so clear that the King assembled his people from everywhere and has left town on 12 March with all his power against the Lanchang people. He made his camp about 5 miles from his enemy, ordering his officers to make one nearer to the enemy." [32]

Two hundred thousand Siamese fought half as many Laotians, the latter led by their king, T'ammikarat (1596-1622). The Laotians were curtly buffeted in a running battle ca. April 5, 1612 (N.S.), suffering many casualties in the vain effort to aggrandize their kingdom at the expense of the Siamese. The king of Laos, hounded by the pursuing Ayudhyans, quitted his elephant to fly on horseback only narrowly escaping capture. The king of Siam, after a successful display of his power, returned to Ayudhya in triumph on April 12th (N.S.). Van Nyenrode states that the Japanese were ordered to depart from the kingdom forthwith.[33] However, notwithstanding van Nyenrode to the contrary, many Japanese did remain in the kingdom, and as we shall see their intrigues kept the Kingdom of Siam in a continual state of agitation.[34] The Japanese were finally expelled from Siam by King Prasat T'ong (1629-56).

The year 1612 was a particularly eventful year in the history of Thailand since, in the same year as the Laotian war, relations were established between Great Britain and Siam. In the seventh voyage sent by the English East India Company to the Indies the *Globe* commanded by Captain Anthony Hippon weighed anchor at Patani June 22, 1612 (O.S.) five years after the first permanent English plantation in the new world. The ship's crew received an honorable reception from the queen of Patani, but the Dutch viewed their arrival with no little trepidation. The English with some difficulty obtained permission to build a factory after the payment of, what they considered, an unreasonable sum.

The British effort to gather the wealth of Siam commenced on an inauspicious note at Patani. The Englishmen were plagued by thieves, and by sickness causing the death of Captain Hippon on July 9th. The English factory, after about ten years of precarious existence, was finally shut down ca. 1622.

Shortly after the arrival of the *Globe* at Patani, Adam Denton, one of the English factors, along with four other companions, journeyed to Ayudhya independently of the *Globe*, and were the first Englishmen to set foot at the capital of Siam. The English factors were greeted in audience by the king of Ayudhya on September 17th. A letter from James I of Great Britain was delivered, and the appearance of the heretofore little known nationality at the court of Ayudhya greatly pleased the king. Each factor received a little golden cup and a piece of cloth in token of friendship. Permission was granted to the English to build a factory at Ayudhya, and to trade throughout the kingdom. The English were nevertheless much embarrassed by the covetousness of Siamese officialdom, and by the unsettled conditions in Siam which interrupted the peaceful flow of trade. Their commercial efforts came to nought, and the factory at Ayudhya was shut down about the same time as the Patani establishment.[35]

The Dutch were not inclined to accept the English with better grace at Ayudhya than their compatriots at Patani.

EXTRACT OF A LETTER FROM CORNELIUS VAN NYENRODE TO HENDRICK
JANSSEN AT PATANI

Dated Judea (Ayudhya), 2nd September 1612 (N.S.)
24th August 1612 (O.S.)

"The English ship has arrived here outside the river, and the merchant called Adam came on the 29th here in the town and directly informed the mandarins that the vessel was outside the town with letters from the King of England, addressed to His Majesty here. Then His Majesty sent Adam with Opra Chula and some prahus [dignitaries] thence yesterday to fetch those letters and the captains, as the King is very much pleased that another nation has arrived in his country; so their (the English) trade cannot be prevented, as you and Lambert Jacobson know very well, that this King tries to attract every nation to his country." [36]

We must now temporarily digress to discuss Burmese affairs before we disclose the salient features of the Siamese-Burman War of 1613-17. After an interregnum of six years (1599-1605), following the death of King Nanda Bayin, Anaukpetlun (1605-28) succeeded his father, the Nyaungyan Prince, as the king of Ava and immediately strove to obtain the supreme kingship of Burma. The Nyaungyan Prince aspired to the supreme kingship, but in the divided state of Burma he was not able to extend his sway beyond the confines of Ava. His son, King Anaukpetlun, was animated not only by the vision of a united Burma, but also opined he could reconstruct the once far-flung imperial edifice which his grandfather, King Bayinnaung, had erected. King Anaukpetlun was not long in seeking to reduce the lesser potentates of Burma to a subordinate status. The Burmese king first extended his authority in the north. In 1608 he captured Prome, and in 1610 he forced the ruler of Toungoo to recognize his supremacy. King Anaukpetlun, in the zealous prosecution of his ambition, was now positioned to unite the lands of the old Kingdom of Pegu to a Burma rising once again from the confusion of its own disunity.[37] The chief obstacle confronting the king of Burma in his Peguan enterprise was the person of the redoubtable Portuguese adventurer—Philip de Brito. De Brito had been sent by the king of Arakan, Minyazagyi (1593-1612), on a mission to Syriam in 1602. In a few years the impulsive and ambitious de Brito had made himself master of the city as an independent sovereign in his own right.[38] De Brito incurred the wrath of his subjects whom he sought to convert to Catholicism by forcible measures. The iconoclastic de Brito plundered the Pagodas long venerated by the Buddhist population. Conciliation of the native element in the population was all the more necessary for the defense of his city, as King Anaukpetlun had determined upon the extirpation of the viper lair and its Lusitanian interloper. The Burmese laid siege to Syriam in 1613 after full preparations. Following a month's siege the city fell to the conquering Burmese[39] (in April 1613),[40] when a Mon chief opened one of the gates. Philip de Brito, a brave but reckless prodigal of Portugal, was cruelly impaled and many of his officers killed by the Burman monarch who showed but a poor regard for the merits of mercy. Binnya (P'ya) Dala, the governor of Martaban for the king of Siam, intimidated by the Burman display of ferocity, submitted to King Anaukpetlun without striking a blow.[41] Thus King Ekat'otsarot, lost the Peguan possessions which his brother, King Naresuen the Black King, had acquired in 1594. The Burmese frontier now extended as far south as the town of Ye.

A sputter of martial activity flared across the Thai-Burmese border for a brief period. The brother of King Anaukpetlun, the prince of Sagaing, was sent to govern Ye. The Siamese governor of Tavoy, in a surprise attack on Ye late in 1613, captured Ye and the Burmese prince. The latter was sent prisoner to Ayudhya. The Burmese retaliated as the conflict swept southward. Tavoy was captured, but the Siamese, with the aid of Portuguese mercenaries, repulsed the attack on Tenasserim in January 1614. The Siamese, according to Wood's version of the campaign, recaptured Tavoy.[42]

The *Hmannan Yazawin Dawgyi* relates a somewhat different story. According to the Burmese chronicle the Burman army arrived at a river (across from Tenasserim), but was unable to cross for lack of boats. The king of Ayudhya, unwilling to passively accept a defensive posture, sought to sever the Burmese communications by felling trees and bamboo. Notwithstanding his stratagem the king of Siam was himself defeated by the Burmese. Burmese history states that after the battle both armies withdrew: the Siamese to Ayudhya and the Burman forces to Mottama (Martaban).[43]

Tharawadi Min,[44] the prince of Chiengmai since 1579 and son of the illustrious Bayinnaung, died about this time, and in the succession disputes which followed his death, King Anaukpetlun thought he saw an opportunity to aggrandize his kingdom. The Burmese invaded Chiengmai, seeking to depose Prince Thadogyaw—precariously holding the reins of government in the turbulent principality. Prince Thadogyaw abandoned Chiengmai, the capital city, but until his death at the siege of Lamp'ang, he was able to prevent the Burmese from making a conquest, in toto, of the Thai state. King Anaukpetlun, once Lamp'ang was in his possession, installed the lord of Nan as a Burmese vassal prince of Chiengmai ca. 1615. The Siamese apparently made no effort to succor their beleaguered vassal. The *Hmannan Yazawin Dawgyi* is silent concerning any Siamese assistance, although Wood suggests an army was sent north, but arrived too late.

Hostilities between Burma and the Kingdom of Ayudhya dragged on inconclusively for a few years until about 1617 when peace was arranged between the two countries. Considering the pusillanimity which the Siamese displayed during the Burmese conquest of Chiengmai, the peace was not unfavorable to Siam. The Siamese abandoned their pretensions to Martaban, while the Burmese relinquished their claim to Chiengmai. The prince of Chiengmai once again came under Siamese tutelage.[45]

EXTRACT OF A LETTER FROM WILLIAM WILSON TO EDWARD LONG,
MERCHANT AT BANTAM

Dated Jakarta, 23rd February 1618 (N.S.?)

". . . that above 3 months past there was a peace between
the king of Siam and the Ava and that the Ava hath yielded
up unto the Siamese Jangama [Chiengmai] and other places
that he had formerly conquered."

The Burmese, however, did not long abide by the agreement. In 1626 the Burmese, while campaigning against the Laotians and people of the surrounding parts, passed through Chiengmai territory, and once again reimposed Burmese suzerainty.[46]

The war with Burma as well as internal disturbances increased the difficulty of peaceful intercourse with the Siamese kingdom. Adam Denton, chief factor of the British factory at Patani, wrote to the English East India Company at the end of 1614 that trade abroad was dead as the result of wars, and that war was feared at Patani with the Acheenders (Acheh). Among the lesser evils at Patani, Denton complains of the lack of paper, ink and books. Even the Chinese paper he was using was eaten through by cockroaches. Denton was not optimistic about the commercial possibilities of Patani. His English countrymen sought to open a factory at Singora, but were blocked by the hostility of the Dutch.[47]

The aggressive Dutchmen, while hindering the English, lost no opportunity to improve their own position at the court of Ayudhya. In June 1617 the Hollanders concluded a treaty with the Siamese king which placed the sale of deer skin, a chief export to Japan, on a secure footing, giving the Dutch an advantage over the English rivals.[48] The Japanese were also aggressive merchants,[49] and their numbers and proximity to the capital were important factors in obtaining Siamese support for their enterprises, commercial or otherwise.

As for the Dutch and English, competition for markets in the orient reached such intensity a trade war developed between the two countries. Two English ships, the *Hound* and *Sampson*, were attacked by three Dutch men-of-war while lying in Patani harbor in July 1619. The English vessels were overwhelmed by the Dutch. The trade war extended even to Japan where some English prisoners, captured by the Dutch, escaped to find sanctuary in an English factory. The Dutch attacked the factory, but were repulsed by the British with Japanese assistance.[50] Peace was eventually restored between England and the Netherlands, but the unsettled conditions in Siam remained unconducive to trade. The English, and apparently the Dutch, closed their factories in Siam ca. 1622.[51] The English ceased to maintain a regular intercourse with the Kingdom of Ayudhya for a period of thirty-seven years. The Dutch apparently reopened the Ayudhya factory in 1624.[52]

King Srey Sauryopor of Cambodia, a vassal of Ayudhya, died in 1618. He was succeeded by Jai Jett'a or Chettha II (1618-25), his eldest son, who proclaimed the independence of Cambodia ca. 1618.[53] No retaliatory action, however, was taken against the rebellious Cambodians until 1622.

King Ekat'otsarot, according to our best surmise, died in 1620.

> "To judge by Siamese records, one might form rather a high opinion of King Ekat'otsarot, but contemporary foreign writers represent him as an odious man, cruel, greedy and suspicious." [54]

II. SRI SAOWAPHAK 1620

The *P'ongsawadan* chronicle states that Sri Saowaphak, the son of Ekat'otsarot, succeeded to the throne of his forbears. King Sri Saowaphak, according to the sometimes unreliable Siamese chronicle, blind in one eye, was executed by one P'ra Sri Sin.[55]

The persuasive Giles states King Sri Saowaphak was murdered by Prince Int'araja, later King Int'araja II or Songt'am (1620-28), and by Phra Ong Lai (Cha-mun Sri Sorarak), later King Prasat T'ong (1629-56), and other noblemen dissatisfied with certain but undesignated conduct of the king.[56] Although Prince Int'araja later expiated his crime (if any), at least in the opinion of his own people, eventually gaining the epithet "The Just King," Phra Ong Lai (Cha-mun Sri Sorarak) steered an abominable course which gained for him the nickname "The Bottled Spider."[57]

III. INT'ARAJA II OR SONGT'AM 1620-28

One of the first acts of King Int'araja II, who raised himself to the throne of Ayudhya over the stricken body of his brother, was to organize an expedition to crush the independence of Cambodia—four years after her declaration of independence. The Siamese rationale in the attempt to subjugate Cambodia is found in the correspondence between Siamese and Japanese dignitaries which, fortunately, has been preserved in Japanese archives.[58] Thai sources are silent about the outcome of the Cambodian War of Independence, perhaps, induced by the fact the advantage lay with the Cambodians.

King Int'araja II in a letter to the Shogun (mistakenly referred to as the king of Japan) sets forth the circumstances of the Cambodian rebellion. The envoys, bearing the letter, arrived at Nagasaki in August 1623. After a short stay the entourage proceeded to Kyoto. On September 24th (N.S.?) they were received by the Shogun Iyemitsu (1623-51) at Fushimi castle.[59] In the extract of the missive printed below, King Int'araja II, the king of Siam, speaks his mind:

EXTRACT OF THE MEMORIAL FROM THE KING OF SIAM TO
THE SHOGUN OF JAPAN

' "Your honoured country and mine being separated by the ocean, we were formerly unable to correspond with each other. But the traffic of merchant ships has now fortunately given me an opportunity, and I am thus enabled to have the honour of friendly communication. . . .

' "Last year I was again disposed to evince my respectful desire of inquiring about you . . . [but could not because of the following circumstances]. The late Prea Srey Sorpor [Srey Sauryopor] of my subject state of Cambodia was loyal and obedient. I had appointed him to govern it, and he discharged his duty well. When he came to die, he enjoined on his son and successor Chesda [Jai Jett'a or Chettha II], the practice of loyal obedience. The latter, however, disregarded the injunctions of his deceased father, and assumed the succession without my sanction. He defied my authority and refused to pay tribute. . . . He has now gone beyond all bounds in the stirring up of trouble; the administration is disorganized, and the people are plunged in distress threatening their utter ruin." ' [60]

King Int'araja II desired the Shogun to admonish Japanese merchants not to traffic with Cambodia or ' ". . . they will run the risk of being hurt in the melee . . ." ' which will not accord with the friendship between the two countries.[61]

Two days later a reply to the letter of King Int'araja II was prepared. The letter, in the name of the former Shogun Hidetada (1605-23), rather condescendingly refers to Int'araja II merely as the Lord of Siam, but otherwise the ex-Shogun affably consents to the most stringent measures against his own Japanese nationals, if as the Thai king judged, Siamese imperial interest necessitated a ruthless prosecution of the war in Cambodia.

EXTRACT OF THE REPLY FROM MINAMOTO HIDETADA OF JAPAN
TO HIS HONOUR THE LORD OF SIAM

Dated, September 1623

' "I must also express my great thanks for the various presents you have sent me. It appears that Cambodia . . . [has] been guilty of discourtesy . . . if merchants of my country resident there should aid them to repel the attack of your honoured country, you wish to exterminate them, although it is not in accordance with the friendly relations existing between Japan and Siam. This will, however, be perfectly just, and you need not hesitate for a moment." ' [62]

Thus Japanese officialdom was already showing that fatal disregard for the benefits of foreign intercourse, a fact which, when combined with the enforced seclusion of the island empire in the 1630s, lasting for more than two hundred years, produced a period of stagnation in Japanese life. Japan, like the Kingdom of Siam in the nineteenth century, stood perilously close to being annexed to one of the expanding empires of the western world. Both countries, however, were able to escape colonial domination by making drastic reforms in the traditional eastern patterns of government and administration. Nothing less than a complete overhaul of the traditional system sufficed to bring both countries in line with the demands of the impinging commercial world of the west. Many Asian states failed to meet the challenge of the new situation, adhering to old systems, incapable of resisting western expansion. These states succumbed to colonial administrations forcedly imposed. China maintained a precarious independence, but only after shattering military defeats inflicted by western nations, and a rejuvenated Japan, did the Chinese begin to take steps to modernize their outmoded and inefficient state organization. The Thai kingdom met the aggressive western world in the only manner possible—by adopting its techniques, and where necessary, those values which heightened western respect for a kingdom (the only state in southeast Asia to escape colonial rule) with the courage and resource to effect necessary transformations, however mortifying to a proud people.

The war with Cambodia was an unqualified failure. The descendants of the ancient Khmers, long fallen from their former grandeur, were nevertheless able to maintain their independence. According to van Vliet * two large armies were sent to Cambodia in 1622. One army moved by water, and the other by land. The naval force was not able to support the land army. The Cambodians, emboldened by the departure of the Thai naval arm, joined battle with the Siamese army. They defeated the invaders by lending the Siamese false guides to lead them from the good roads of the country into low fields. The Thais were victims of a well concealed ambush. Van Vliet states the Siamese left the Cambodians in peace, although they made preparations from time to time for renewed attacks.[63]

In 1624 the Portuguese and Spanish suffered a further diminution of influence at the court of Ayudhya. The Spaniards captured a Dutch yacht in Siamese waters, a deed which greatly offended His Siamese Majesty. The Portuguese, subject to the same king as the Spanish, Philip IV (1621-65), incurred apparently because of the Spanish connection, the same disfavor as their fellow Iberians. The Portuguese were never again to regain their former influence at the Ayudhyan court. In fact the Portuguese had fallen on such bad times that King Prasat T'ong (1629-56), the usurper of ill repute, of which more will be said, kept many Portuguese in captivity forcing them to "go about begging in the streets."[64] The decline of Portuguese influence at Ayudhya corresponded with a rise of the Dutch in importance in the kingdom. The European rivals of the Dutch at Ayudhya were either in disfavor, as were the Portuguese, or were temporarily out of business, as were the English.

King Int'araja II died about April 1628.[65] The "Just King" was not of a warlike disposition, and he engaged his time largely in study, religious pursuits and the improvement of the laws of his kingdom. King Int'araja II was only thirty-eight at the time of his death.

> "He was generous to the priests and to the poor, and repaired
> or constructed more temples than any previous King. He
> kept great state, and liked to see his nobles live magnifi-
> cently. Foreigners and Siamese alike sang his praises, and re-
> garded him as a good and just ruler, almost as a saint. Siam
> was not to see his like again for many years."[66]

As King Int'araja II lay dying, Phra Ong Lai who had become P'ya Sri

---

* Chief Dutch factor at Ayudhya 1636-41.

Worawong (apparently the title for the Chamberlain of the Household) concurred in the wish of Int'araja II to place the sovereign's son on the Siamese throne. Prince Sri Sin, a brother of the king and bitter enemy of Phra Ong Lai (P'ya Sri Worawong), was also a claimant to the kingship and regarded by many Thais as a more suitable candidate to discharge the weighty responsibilities of the kingship of Siam. Although the Phra Ong Lai (P'ya Sri Worawong) fell in with the king's wishes as regards the succession to the throne, the suggestion nevertheless has been made that he hastened the death of King Int'araja II by administering poison,[67] an act certainly in keeping with the general tone of the moral life of the ambitious minister. The death of King Int'araja II ushered in a period of confusion such as seldom had been seen in Siam, lasting well into the 1630s.

IV. JETT'A (CHETTHATHIRAT) 1628-29

King Jett'a, the son of Int'araja II, was a boy of fifteen at the time of his accession to the throne and a mere puppet of Phra Ong Lai (P'ya Sri Worawong), the ambitious and abominable minister—shortly to raise himself to the throne of Ayudhya. King Jett'a was set on the throne in opposition to the claim of Prince Sri Sin, who had probably been appointed the Maha Uparat in the previous reign, since foreign writers assert that he was the lawful heir to the throne. Phra Ong Lai (P'ya Sri Worawong) commenced a reign of terror against his enemies. P'ya Kalahom (Minister of the Military Division) and many of his supporters suffered death crossing the path of the malign ambition of Phra Ong Lai (P'ya Sri Worawong). P'ya Kalahom and his followers were executed by order of the king on the advice of Phra Ong Lai (P'ya Sri Worawong) since they favored the claim of Prince Sri Sin to the kingship of Siam. Phra Ong Lai (P'ya Sri Worawong) induced King Jett'a to appoint him to the title and office of the now vacant P'ya Kalahom.[68]

Phra Ong Lai (now P'ya Kalahom) had made himself the mortal enemy of Prince Sri Sin by intriguing with his wives, and the dissipated minister realized his own life was forfeit if Prince Sri Sin ascended the throne. Nor had the minister improved his relations with Prince Sri Sin by entering a plot with four bosom companions to murder the prince. Phra Ong Lai (P'ya Kalahom) had, as a consequence, readily supported the efforts of Int'araja II to raise his son to the throne of Ayudhya.[69]

Prince Sri Sin, with a view to assuring his own safety, took the precaution of becoming a Buddhist priest about the time Jett'a became the king of Siam. Prince Sri Sin, however, remained an ever present danger to the ambitions of Phra Ong Lai (P'ya Kalahom). The prince had many supporters who believed he had a just claim to the kingship, and the young king undoubtedly realized his own throne would never be secure as long as Prince Sri Sin was willing to dispute his title. The P'ya Kalahom therefore proposed a solution. He enlisted the support of the Japanese headman, Yamada, to murder Prince Sri Sin. Yamada, who had supported Int'araja II, in his dying wish to place his son on the throne, promised to bring the prince not only to court, but to bring Prince Sri Sin to court in secular dress, since in the garb of an ecclesiastic no one, perhaps not even the Kalahom, dared to lay a malevolent finger on him. Yamada, in pursuance of his scheme, visited the prince offering to support his claim to the kingship of Siam. The dissimulating Yamada induced Prince Sri Sin to leave his sanctuary and go to court to deprive King Jett'a of his crown with Japanese assistance. Prince Sri Sin, against advice to the contrary, all too readily trusted the wily Yamada.

Yamada induced the prince, as they approached the royal palace, to remove his ecclesiastical robe and don the attire of a prince in order to present a bold front to the world and convince his countrymen that he was a man of resolve and action. The prince complied with the request of Yamada. Prince Sri Sin, Yamada and some of his Japanese henchmen entered the royal palace. The betrayed prince was immediately seized, bound and brought before King Jett'a (probably with a gloating P'ya Kalahom at his side). The king thanked Yamada for his services to the crown.

Prince Sri Sin was condemned to death, and was placed in a dry well at P'etchaburi (Phet Buri) to perish of starvation.* Mongkhol, a relation of the prince, was able to rescue Prince Sri Sin by digging a mine communicating with the well. The corpse of a slave was placed in the well, dressed in the clothes of the prince. Prince Sri Sin, who was at death's door, was thus rescued. The guards, thinking the prince was dead, filled the well, and paying last honors to the prince sent notice of Prince Sri Sin's certain death to Ayudhya. At the dissolute court of King Jett'a: "This news caused there so universal a joy that the King and his Minister imagined there was no longer anything which could trouble the repose of the Kingdom, and flung themselves into a strange security." [70]

Prince Sri Sin, restored to health, raised an army of twenty thousand men, and had himself proclaimed king of Siam at Pipry (P'etchaburi). Although taken by surprise, the depraved court was not unequal to the exigencies of the new situation. An army, also of about twenty thousand men, was quickly raised and placed under the command of P'ya Kamhaen. Yamada accompanied the expedition with seven or eight hundred of his intrepid Japanese soldiery. On arriving at Pipry (P'etchaburi) both sides engaged in frequent skirmishes, but no general engagement was fought. Yamada, the archdeceiver, once again employed his subtle arts on the trusting Prince Sri Sin. The Japanese headman advertised he was deserting the royal cause, and following several conferences with representatives of Prince Sri Sin, agreed his forces should mock charge those of the prince. Yamada, and apparently a relatively large portion of the army of Prince Sri Sin, agreed not to employ bullets. The Japanese feigning defeat would then surrender themselves to Prince Sri Sin. Yamada was untrue to his word. The Japanese, powerfully seconded by the Thai troops of the royal army, attacked the army of Prince Sri Sin with all the paraphernalia of war. The troops of the prince were taken by surprise. The prince withdrew toward Ligor. A second battle was fought on the way south, and the results were equally unfortunate for Prince Sri Sin. The hapless prince was taken prisoner before reaching Ligor. [71]

Prince Sri Sin could expect no mercy from the clique into whose hands he had fallen. He was beaten to death with a sandalwood club in the prescribed manner for princes of the blood. One wonders why such a "conventional" mode of execution was not adopted in the first instance.

---

* The fastidious Jett'a did not wish to be responsible for the shedding of royal blood.

45

With one more rival eliminated "The Bottled Spider" was slowly but efficaciously spinning a web to enmesh all his victims. He envisioned clearly his goal—the throne of Siam, and determined to secure the object of his ambition if necessary with measured doses of venom seditiously injected at opportune moments. The P'ya Kalahom encouraged King Jett'a to bemuse himself in a life of idleness and dissipation as a means of bringing the monarch into general disfavor. A crisis was reached in the relations between the king and his abandoned minister. P'ya Kalahom had been gradually usurping the trappings of royalty. The limit of the young king's patience was reached when "The Bottled Spider" cremated a deceased relative in a style reserved for the greatest personages. The jealousy of the young king, pitted against the ambitious minister, was thoroughly aroused. The king made violent threats against P'ya Kalahom.[72]

King Jett'a was planning to arrest the P'ya Kalahom, but was himself surprised by the vigor of the minister's response when the latter attacked the palace forcing the young king to flee. King Jett'a was captured, and executed by the P'ya Kalahom who had the presumption to declare the king merited death for deserting his high office! [73]

King Jett'a apparently died in 1629. Siamese history states the king reigned for nineteen months. Giles places the date of his execution in September 1629.[74]

V. AT'ITYAWONG 1629

P'ya Kalahom, notwithstanding the success of his machinations, was not yet able to sit in the royal chair. His accomplice in deeds of inequity, Yamada, advocated that the ten year old brother of King Jett'a, Prince At'ityawong, ascend the throne. The P'ya Kalahom, fearful of antagonizing Yamada and the turbulent Japanese, agreed not to accept kingship but the regency of the young prince. In the new capacity, the regent did not eschew his old ways, executing P'ya Kamhaen, the commander of the royal troops, who "The Bottled Spider" feared would resent his appointment to the regency. This crime greatly angered Yamada, the companion in arms of P'ya Kamhaen, but the crafty P'ya Kalahom by acts of conciliation reduced Yamada to a more amenable frame of mind. The Japanese leader was appointed to the governorship of Nakhon Sri Thamarat (Ligor). By such means the P'ya Kalahom was able to remove his Japanese adversaries from the precincts of the capital to a less threatening position in the south. Yamada, an intriguer of no little adeptness himself, was lulled by a promise of the regent that no harm would come to the young king.[75] With Yamada and his Japanese soldiers safely out of the way, the regent was able to act with a freer hand. The ten year old king was tumbled from the throne, and clubbed to death after a reign of little more than a month.[76] The young king:

> ". . . piteously denounced the cruelty of the man who had set
> him on a throne only to deprive him of his life; but there
> was no mercy to be expected from a monster who knew no
> law but his own ambition." [77]

"The Bottled Spider" had closed the web of his intrigue over the last person who blocked his way to the kingship of Siam. Yamada on hearing of the execution was furious but powerless. When the P'ya Kalahom assumed the throne under the title of Prasat T'ong, Yamada dissembled his true feelings, expressing his loyalty and fidelity to the new king.[78] Yamada, as we shall see in the next chap-

46

ter, was himself to fall victim to King Prasat T'ong, after "The Bottled Spider" commenced to wave the blood-spattered sceptre of Siam in his own forsaken style.

BIBLIOGRAPHY

1. Anderson, John. *English Intercourse with Siam in the Seventeenth Century*, Kegan Paul, Trench, Trubner, & Co., Ltd., London, 1890.
2. Blankwaardt, W. "Notes upon the Relations between Holland and Siam," *Journal of the Siam Society*, Vol. VII, Bangkok, 1959.
3. Chula, H.R.H. Prince. *Lords of Life*, Taplinger Publishing Co., Inc., New York, 1960.
4. Giles, Francis H. "A Critical Analysis of Van Vliet's Historical Account of Siam in the 17th Century," *Journal of the Siam Society*, Vol. VII, Bangkok, 1959.
5. Hall, D. G. E. *A History of South-East Asia*, MacMillan & Co., Ltd., London, and St. Martin's Press, New York, 1961.
6. Hutchinson, E. W. *Adventures in Siam in the Seventeenth Century*, The Royal Asiatic Society, London, 1940.
7. "Intercourse between Burma and Siam, as recorded in Hmannan Yazawindawgyi," *Journal of the Siam Society*, Vol. V, Part 1, Bangkok, 1959.
8. *Records of the Relations between Siam and Foreign Countries in the 17th Century*, Printed by order of the Council of the Vajiranana National Library, Vol. I, Bangkok, 1915.
9. Satow, E. M. "Notes on the Intercourse between Japan and Siam," *Transactions of the Asiatic Society of Japan*, Vol. XIII, Yokohama, 1885.
10. Turpin, François Henri. *History of the Kingdom of Siam*, Printed under auspices of the Committee of the Vajiranana National Library, Bangkok, 1908. English translation by Cartwright, B. O.
11. Van Vliet, Jeremias. "Description of the Kingdom of Siam," *Journal of the Siam Society*, Vol. VII, Part 1, Bangkok, 1910. English translation by van Ravenswaay, L. F.
————. "Historical Account of Siam," *Journal of the Siam Society*, Vol. VII, Bangkok, 1959. English translation by Mundie, W. H.
12. Wood, W. A. R. *A History of Siam*, The Siam Barnakich Press, Bangkok, 1933.

FOOTNOTES

1. Hall, 297.
2. Ibid., 228.
3. Blankwaardt, 14-16.
4. Hall, 233, 234.
5. Blankwaardt, 17, 18. Giles states that Warwyck (Waerwijck) sent an individual named Specx to Ayudhya as his envoy implying that van Warwyck himself did not go; See Giles, 96.
6. Hall, 297. Anderson states the embassy was received in 1608; See Anderson, 38. Hutchinson, using an entry from the minutes of the Dutch East India Company, places the reception of the embassy in 1609; See Hutchinson, 27.
7. Giles, 111.
8. Blankwaardt, 18.

9. Anderson, 37, 38.
10. Hutchinson, 23.
11. Records, etc., 3, 4.
12. Hall, 299.
13. Blankwaardt, 19; Consult also *The Portugues Asia* of Manuel de Faria y Sousa, 1590-1649, Vol. III.
14. Wood, 158.
15. Ibid.
16. The following authorities state or imply that King Ekat'otsarot died in 1610: Wood, 160; Prince Chula, 52, and Hall, 317.
17. Giles, 111, and Records, etc., 101.
18. Wood, 128.
19. Ibid., 160.
20. Giles, 111, 112. The document is believed to have been written about 1622, because mention is made of troubles in Cambodia. King Int'araja II undertook an invasion of Cambodia in 1622. The document itself has been badly damaged.
21. Records, etc., 139.
22. Wood, 159, 160. Turpin, 1709-99, whose *History of the Kingdom of Siam* was first published in 1771, states: "The King misled by the representations of his favourite pronounced sentence of death on his innocent son . . ."; See Turpin, 23. Giles also states his belief that the king's son was executed, but assigns the event to the year 1612; See Giles, 118.
23. Giles, 115.
24. Ibid., 116.
25. Ibid.
26. Wood, 159, 160.
27. Ibid., 160, 161. Giles describes a Japanese revolt in 1620 in terms which are nearly identical with those used by Wood to describe the revolt which I have placed about the year 1611. Giles, although allowing for the fact that the Japanese revolted ca. 1611 or 1612, states they revolted again during the reign of the next king of Siam, Sri Saowaphak (1620), whose kingship is doubted by some authorities. Wood for his presentation has apparently relied on the account of Peter Floris—a contemporary of the period. Giles also uses Floris, among other authorities, to support his view that the Japanese forced concessions from King Sri Saowaphak. But Floris died in 1615. Therefore Floris could not have described events taking place in 1620, but if they took place at all the date must be assigned to a year before 1615; See Giles, 145-48; Consult also the Journal of Peter Floris, d. 1615.
28. Wood, 161.
29. Hall, 299.
30. Wood, 161.
31. Giles believes that Chao Fa Tana is no other than Prince Sut'at, and that his questionable communication with the Lanchang people (Laotians) was the cause of his execution on suspicion of disloyalty; See Giles, 117, 118.
32. Records, etc., 6, 7.
33. Ibid., 7, 8.
34. "Prince Damrong has suggested the following very probable explanation

of the favour shown to the Japanese, in spite of their excesses. There were a number of peaceable Japanese settlers in Siam, from among whom the bodyguard was recruited. There was also a gang of more or less piratical "birds of passage". . . [such as had raised the revolt]. . . . They were probably expelled from the Kingdom, doubtless with the aid of their more loyal fellow-countrymen.

"At that time Japanese pirates were a pest all over the Far East. In December 1605 the English navigator, John Davis, lost his life in a fight with Japanese pirates off Patani. In the same year, and again in 1610, the King of Cambodia complained to the Shogun of Japan of the acts of piracy committed by Japanese traders in his realm."; See Wood, 162.

35. Anderson, 47-50; Consult the Journal of Peter Floris.
36. Records, etc., 9.
37. Hall, 316.
38. Wood, 163; Consult also Faria y Sousa, Vol. III.
39. Hall, 316.
40. Wood, 164.
41. Hall, 316, 317.
42. Wood, 164.
43. "Intercourse, etc.," 160.
44. Different years are given for the death of Tharawadi Min. The *Hmannan Yazawin Dawgyi* states that the prince of Chiengmai died after King Anaukpetlun had retired to Mottama (Martaban) ca. 1614; See "Intercourse, etc.," 160. Wood states that Tharawadi Min died in 1607; See Wood, 164, 165.
45. Wood, 165, 166.
46. Records, etc., 89, and Wood, 169.
47. Anderson, 58, 59.
48. Ibid., 67, and Hall, 300.
49. Anderson, 72.
50. Ibid., 74-77.
51. Ibid., 84-86.
52. Hall, 300, and Giles, 97.
53. Wood, 166.
54. Ibid., 160.
55. Ibid.
56. Giles, 100, 101.
57. Wood vigorously denies that Sri Saowaphak was ever king of Siam. For his arguments; See Wood, 160. I have included Sri Saowaphak among the kings of Siam, relying on the *P'ongsawadan*, Giles and the authority of Prince Damrong.
58. Giles, 127.
59. Satow, 156.
60. Ibid., 156, 157.
61. Ibid., 157.
62. Ibid., 158.
63. Van Vliet, "Description, etc.," 35, 36.
64. Ibid., 52, 53.
65. Giles, 124. Wood states the king died December 22, 1628; See Wood, 170, 171.

66. Wood, 170, 171.
67. Giles, 101.
68. Wood, 170, 172.
69. Giles, 101.
70. Van Vliet, "Historical Account, etc.," 37-40.
71. Ibid., 40-42.
72. Wood, 174.
73. Giles, 126.
74. Ibid., 113.
75. Ibid., 170-72.
76. Wood, 175.
77. Ibid.
78. Giles, 173.

CHAPTER THREE

THE LATE AYUDHYA PERIOD 1629 - 1767 — PART 1
UNTIL THE REVOLUTION OF 1688

I. PRASAT T'ONG 1629-56

King Prasat T'ong, bespotted, by stains of avarice, ambition and the blood of his conquests, late in the year 1629 commenced to sway, in the shadow of his own inequity, the royal sceptre of Siam. His reign is a catalogue of violent actions bedazzled by repeated acts of royal buffoonery. The kingship of "The Bottled Spider" also marks an eclipse in the reputation as well as the external influence of the Kingdom of Siam as rebellions disturbed the internal repose of the kingdom, while the Dutch threatened to upset the external equilibrium following the expulsion of the Japanese from Siam in 1632.

King Prasat T'ong certainly occupied a very isolated position at the commencement of his reign. The Japanese were at enmity with the usurper, notwithstanding professions of loyalty from Yamada. Neither the Shogun of Japan among foreign rulers, nor the vassal queen of Patani recognized the title of "The Bottled Spider," and the violence and cruelty the king displayed were not calculated to win him popular affection.

The aggressive Japanese, for many years past a threat to the security of Siam, loomed large in the fevered calculations of King Prasat T'ong (who sought to bridle their domineering license). The king of Ayudhya, ever mistrustful of potential rivals, eliminated Yamada, Nipponese enemy number one, by means of poison (1629), shortly after the latter had assumed the governorship of Nak'on Srit'ammarat (Ligor). Oin Yamada, the son of the Japanese leader, retired to Cambodia, but after a short interval reappeared at Ayudhya. The wary King Prasat T'ong, decided to be rid of the Japanese menace once and for all.

"The Japanese quarter of Ayut'ia was suddenly attacked by night, during the flood season of 1632 [ca. October 1632]. Many of the Japanese were ruthlessly butchered, but a large number of them escaped by boat. They were pursued by the Siamese, and a sharp fight was kept up from Ayut'ia down to the sea, with heavy losses on both sides. The majority of the Japanese made good their escape to Cambodia." [1]

The vassal queen of Patani denounced King Prasat T'ong for his villainies, and refused to send the accustomed tribute. The city of Nak'on Srit'ammarat (Ligor) also rebelled against the king of Siam. The king, in a blaze of fury, led an expedition against the recalcitrants of Ligor ca. 1632 destroying the city, and removing most of the inhabitants to Ayudhya in the wake of his ill humor. An expedition against Patani (in 1632 or 1633) was repulsed by the Patanese. King Prasat T'ong blamed the Dutch for the failure of the expedition since the latter were expected to assist with two ships. The Dutch, however, did not proffer the expected assistance. In 1634 about fifty thousand troops, dispatched by land and sea, sought to bring the Patanese to a due respect for the power of the king of Siam. The Dutch promised naval support. The campaign, however, suffered from the effects of mismanagement. The Siamese did not wait for the arrival of the Dutch fleet. The attack on Patani was repulsed, and a shortage of provisions obliged the Siamese to retire on Singora. When the Dutch arrived at the place of rendezvous the Hollanders found the Siamese had departed. A reconciliation between King Prasat T'ong and the queen of Patani, however, was effected through Dutch mediation in 1636. The upshot being that Patanese envoys presented the customary gold and silver tree in token of tributary status.[2]

The Dutch, notwithstanding a sluggishness in aiding the schema of King Prasat T'ong, remained the only foreign friends of the Ayudhyan king. Prince Frederick Henry (1625-47), the Dutch stadtholder, dispatched a letter to King Prasat T'ong confirming Dutch-Siamese bonds of friendship.

EXTRACT OF THE LETTER FROM THE PRINCE OF ORANGE TO THE KING OF SIAM
Dated ca. 1635

"Friedrich by the Grace of God Prince of Orange, Count
of Nassau & c. & c. Captain General and Admiral of the
United Netherlands
Wishes
to the mighty King of Siam in the city of Judea, long
life, health, a prosperous reign and victory over his enemies.

"We have received by our ships recently arrived from the
East Indies your Majesty's agreeable and valuable letters together with accompanying gifts from your Majesty's royal
city, presented to us by the captain of the fleet, whereby we
clearly perceive your Majesty's particular royal affection and
love to our Netherland nation, with frank declaration and
testimony of your Majesty's good will towards the maintenance of the old alliance and correspondence between your
Majesty's Kingdom and this state, which we esteem and value
as highly as anything in the world. With reference to which
we also find ourselves bound hereby to assure your Majesty
again, that as long as the world lasts we and our successors
will always maintain these relations inviolate and un-
changed." [3]

King Prasat T'ong, however, was not long in finding grave fault with the Dutch. Differences with reference to a rice consignment destined for the Dutch governor-general of the East Indies miffed the king. Then in December 1636 two Dutch employees, quarreling with members of the Buddhist priesthood, precipitated a brawl. The next day the Dutchmen were charged with attacking the house of the king's brother. King Prasat T'ong sentenced two members of the Dutch community to be trampled to death by elephants as retribution for the misdemeanors of others. Van Vliet, Dutch factor 1636-41, by the judicious distribution of presents to the king and principal officials, secured the release of the prisoners, although not until they had been bound hand and foot, and exposed to the ridicule of the public. Van Vliet was obliged to sign a state-ment binding the Dutch in Siam to obey the orders of the P'rak'lang (Minister of the Treasury). King Prasat T'ong, who among his many vices numbered drunkenness, was drunk at this ceremony.[4]

March 1638 marked the commencement of the year 1000 of the Chulasa-karat Era. The superstitious king was convinced a dreadful calamity awaited mankind unless changes were made in the Siamese (as well as the Burmese) calendar. As a solvent the king of Siam proposed to change the year sequence from the year of the Tiger (1638-39 A.D.) to the year of the Pig.* King Prasat T'ong wrote to the king of Burma, Thalun (1629-48), suggesting the adoption of the chimerical plan in that country. The Burman king refused to countenance such a proposal. Upon receiving the Burman embassy bearing the unfavorable reply, King Prasat T'ong, in a fury, dismissed the emissaries with insults. Nor did King Prasat T'ong's pet reform win acceptance in Siam.[5]

In 1639 a serious altercation with King Prasat T'ong again threatened the safety of the Dutch in the Kingdom of Ayudhya. The Dutch East India Company claimed a debt against the king, who blew hot and cold over meeting his financial obligations. Van Vliet used strong language expressing the Dutch point of view, and the report was current van Vliet uttered a threat to bring the Dutch fleet to Ayudhya if King Prasat T'ong did not comply with the Dutch demands.

"The King, who was, as usual, drunk when this report was made to him, at first ordered the immediate execution of every Dutchman in Siam. He was induced to grant them one day's grace in which to leave the country, failing which they were to be trampled to death by elephants, and the factory given up to plunder. The whole capital was thrown into confusion. Troops were called out, cannon pointed at the Dutch factory, and all the Dutchmen were arrested and kept in confinement for some time." [6]

The fickle king, however, changed his mind (perhaps sobered by reflections of his own impotence), releasing the confined Dutchmen, and even bestowing marks of favor on van Vliet. In November 1641 King Prasat T'ong received a letter from the Prince of Orange. "The King received the Prince's letter in an unusually ceremonious manner, and said that he had never before been favoured with so pleasing a missive." Nevertheless Dutch relations with Siam remained strained, and van Vliet continued an advocate of aggressive action to bring King Prasat T'ong to a more amenable frame of mind.[7]

Siamese relations with the vassal state of Kedah, under the vagaries of threatened war with the Rajah of Kedah, settled in a happy repose in 1644 to the satisfaction of Dutch mercantile interests as revealed in the following letter:

EXTRACT OF THE LETTER FROM JEREMIAS VAN VLIET
TO GOVERNOR ARNOLD HEUSSEN
Dated Malacca,** 13th October 1644 (N.S.)
3rd October 1644 (O.S.)

"The King of Siam has been for some time threatening to make war on Queda [Kedah], because Rajah Queda has

---

* The twelve-year cycle includes the year of: 1) The Rat, 2) The Ox, 3) The Tiger, 4) The Hare, 5) The Dragon, 6) The Serpent, 7) The Horse, 8) The Goat, 9) The Monkey, 10) The Cock, 11) The Dog and 12) The Pig.
** The Dutch captured Malacca from the Portuguese in January 1641.

ascended the throne at his father's death without permission of the King of Siam and refuses to recognize his superiority. The trade of the Company suffers greatly from this unsettled state of affairs. . . . Rajah Queda is a very young man. He employs his people in building fortresses at every point of his kingdom for fear of the King of Siam, so that the tin mining industry has been greatly interfered with. A large number of the inhabitants have also left the country for fear of the disturbances. However, the disputes between the Kings have been adjusted. Rajah Queda has sent Ambassadors to Siam with valuable presents and the ambassadors from Siam have come to Queda to point out to the king his faults and receive his promise to behave better in [the] future. Peace has been re-established and we now hope that the tin industry will revive." [8]

Having quenched the fires of revolt in Patani (1636) and doused the embers of incipient rebellion in Kedah (1644), King Prasat T'ong discovered Singora ready to dispute the ill-favored royal credentials. In 1648 King Prasat T'ong dispatched an expedition to subdue the rebels of Singora.[9] The Dutch were willing to proffer their assistance not unnaturally with a mind to accruing benefits in the Dutch commercial interest.

EXTRACT OF THE INSTRUCTIONS TO COMMANDER ABEL JANSEN TASMAN
FROM THE COUNCIL AT BATAVIA

Dated, 14th May 1648 (N.S.)
4th May 1648 (O.S.)

"You will . . . proceed straight to Sangora [Singora] which is now besieged by the King of Siam's fleet, and His Majesty has desired our assistance so that he may incorporate it with his kingdom. You must therefore spare no effort to reach that place since a great service would be thus rendered to the King and, in consequence, many substantial benefits would be secured for the [Dutch] Company." [10]

No records remain describing the outcome of the expedition to Singora, or whether, in fact, the Dutch actually participated. We may infer, however, that the expedition failed in purpose since ca. 1654-55 Dutch and Siamese relations once again were frayed by the Dutch failure to provide assistance against the rebels of Singora.

EXTRACT OF A NOTE FROM THE COUNCIL AT BATAVIA
TO THE DUTCH EAST INDIA COMPANY

Dated, 18th January 1655 (N.S.)
8th January 1655 (O.S.)

"It appears that the merchant Hendrich Craijer Zalr had promised, so they say, 20 ships, which was a very rash proceeding on his part, and thereupon they made the above-mentioned expedition [against the rebels of Singora], which they said, if our support did not appear, would be obliged to return unsuccessful and with shame and dishonour to the crown, as was actually the case . . . [Moreover] . . . Westerwolt [Chief Dutch factor] had on various occasions made complaint of the bad and unreasonable treatment received, but got nothing by it but a summons to court, and before four Ojas or councillors was questioned on certain points to which he had to answer forthwith, and the answer was written down word for word, to be laid before the King, who sat by and waited, and every now and then asked whether one of the question[s] had yet been put. So that the resident was in very great embarrassment and did not know whether even his life was any longer safe. These questions were for the most part on the subject of the help asked for against Sangora . . ." [11]

King Prasat T'ong was told the Dutch war with England * precluded dispatch of any ships to help in the suppression of the rebellion. The anger of "The Bottled Spider" was mollified by conveyance of many valuable presents. The Siamese army, which had been waiting at Nak'on Srit'ammarat (Ligor) for Dutch assistance, received orders of recall, and the unfortunate commander was cast in irons,[12] although the intervention of the king's sons and others procured his release.** [13]

In March 1655, King Prasat T'ong beat the war drums, launching another expedition against the rebels of Singora.

EXTRACT OF A NOTE FROM THE COUNCIL AT BATAVIA
TO THE DUTCH EAST INDIA COMPANY

Dated, 27th December 1655 (N.S.)
17th December 1655 (O.S.)

"The Siamese King has resumed the war with Sangora [Singora] and in March last had again a powerful force both on land and sea there. He has, however, effected as little as before, since the admiral who had undertaken to overcome the place with the naval force ran away, so that they returned to Siam with shame." [14]

The revolt of Singora seems to have lasted until 1679 when the city finally submitted to Siamese rule.[15]

King Prasat T'ong, usurper, tyrant and murderer; scurrilous, false and fickle as he was; nevertheless, incongruous as it may seem, is associated in Thai history with a number of beneficial laws. But intolerance in the unbalanced mind of "The Bottled Spider" found expression in penalties enacted against Thais who, marrying foreigners, were converted to a religion other than Buddhism. Such apostates were threatened with confiscation of property, fines and persons so renouncing the old religion were menaced with imprisonment for life.

' "Why is this? Because the (foreign) father will sow seed

---

* First Anglo-Dutch War, May 1652-April 1654
** The royal forces apparently engaged in no fighting during the expedition.

and beget future progeny, and the father and son will report the affairs of the Realm in foreign lands, and when they became [become] known, foreigners will assail the Realm on every side, and the Buddhist religion will decline and fall into disrepute." ' [16]

Although King Prasat T'ong discriminated against Christianity as well as other non-Buddhist religions, the small Thai Christian community did not experience the cruel persecution which, for instance, the Japanese Shogunate (also mistrusting the loyalty of native Christians) imposed seeking to extirpate the Christian religion in the interest of the Japanese state during the same century. Indeed King Narai (1656-88) showered many favors on Catholic missionaries who during his reign attempted the conversion of the Kingdom of Ayudhya.

King Prasat T'ong, during his reign, erected a temple (patterned along the majestic lines of Angkor Thom in Cambodia) on the road from Ayudhya to P'rabat. Wood speculates the king of Ayudhya erected the temple to celebrate the return of Cambodia to allegiance after her declaration of independence in 1618. No record can be found of a Thai invasion of Cambodia during the reign of King Prasat T'ong, but Wood declares that a show of force was probably sufficient to induce the Cambodians to accept Siamese vassalage.[17]

The violent life of the obdurate king reached its infamous term on August 8, 1656 (O.S.).[18]

"It seems strange that this man, who had obtained the throne of Siam through intrigue and murder, and had retained it by methods of terrorism, was allowed to die quietly in bed. Not only this, but he even seems to have been regarded by some contemporary and later writers with a certain degree of admiration. Van Schouten speaks of him as "ruling with great reputation and honour," and the compilers of the Siamese P'ongsawadan apparently had rather a high opinion of him. He was evidently one of those successful upstarts who succeed, by sheer force of audacity, in impressing upon others a false opinion of their merits. If there was anything really great about the man, it certainly is not evident in the accounts of contemporary observers." [19]

II. CHAO FA JAI 1656

The violent succession disputes, culminating in the rise to power of Prasat T'ong, marring the tranquility and repose of the Kingdom of Ayudhya, were by no means assuaged during the remaining years of the next half century. Violence, intrigue and murder associated with the succession disputes of the period signalize a decline and demoralization of the Kingdom of Ayudhya following the heroic age of King Naresuen. A certain contempt of the Thais is discernible among many European writers of the late Ayudhya period. For instance European observers express a low regard for Thai valor, whereas during the reign of King Naresuen the Thais were recognized as good soldiers. The poor showing of the royal army against rebellious but small Singora exemplifies the inefficiency which had overtaken this branch of the Siamese military service. The kings of Ayudhya were unable to rally a response in the chords of Thai hearts as in former years. Such kings as Prasat T'ong (1629-56) and P'rachao Sua (1703-09) reeked inequity, disgraced as they were by the foulness of their crimes. Other Thai kings of the later Ayudhya period, although not sunk in a mire of equal vice, were nevertheless far from being men worthy of emulation. True the kings of Siam during the later Ayudhya period were not altogether devoid of character, witness King P'etraja (1688-1703) whose patriotic impulses directed him to successfully rally the forces dedicated to the maintenance of the independence of his country. Nevertheless the remaining kings of Ayudhya strike a lesser pose than their famous predecessors. No monarch of the renown of King Naresuen (1590-1605) steps forward to win our applause for masterful application of the military art. No king of Ayudhya deserves encomiums in the field of administration such as we might bestow on King Trailok (1448-88). Lastly no king of Ayudhya of the late Ayudhya period is able to master our affections as King Rama Khamheng (1275-1317) whose magnanimity, resource and good sense made the great Sukhothai king a father to his people. The kings of Ayudhya who followed the innocent At'ityawong (1629) as a group are remarkable less for their accomplishments than for depravity and vindictiveness, and by comparison with Rama Khamheng, Trailok and Naresuen are pale shadows standing in the shade of monarchs of greater stature.

Chao Fa Jai, the eldest son of Prasat T'ong, seized the throne of Siam although Sri Sut'ammaraja, the younger brother of Prasat T'ong, had been appointed the Maha Uparat.[20] The new king ruled for a few days only. He was deposed by Sri Sut'ammaraja and Prince Narai, and executed. Sri Sut'ammaraja ascended the throne of Ayudhya while Prince Narai waited in the anteroom, so to speak, having acquired the title of the Maha Uparat.[21]

III. SRI SUT'AMMARAJA 1656

King Sri Sut'ammaraja ruled Siam for three months, his character being as baleful as his brother's. In November 1656 King Sri Sut'ammaraja, captivated by the charms of his niece, the sister of Prince Narai, made amorous advances to the princess offensive to her sense of decorum. The distressed princess, to preserve a lady's honor, had to be whisked by friends from the enamoured clutches of her uncle in a bookcase smuggled from the palace. The royal lady complained to her brother, Prince Narai, of the flagrancy of the king's error. Prince Narai reacted by dethroning his uncle. The palace was stormed by Prince Narai and his cohorts, and although King Sri Sut'ammaraja escaped immediate capture, suffering a wound in the neck, he was apprehended a few days later and executed.[22]

IV. NARAI 1656-88

King Narai ascended the throne of Siam in blood and violence, not out of keeping with the abased standards of the late Ayudhya monarchy. The young king (ca. twenty-five years of age) signalized the advent of a new and portentous reign for Siam, by executing two younger brothers accused of plotting against his life. Other suspects were also executed.[23]

The field of foreign affairs, however, forms the subject of foremost interest in Thai history during the reign of King Narai. The tempo of foreign intervention in Siam increased during King Narai's long and eventful reign, climaxing in 1687-88 with the military expedition sent by Louis XIV, king of France, ostensibly to protect Thailand from the Dutch, but in reality to dominate the Kingdom of Siam in the interest of France. We shall see the Thais were equal to the exigencies posed by the French threat to the independence of Siam rallying to the patriotic if not overly scrupulous P'etraja (1688-1703).

The renewed foreign interest in Thailand commenced in 1659 when the English factory in Cambodia was looted during civil disturbances in that country, and the Englishmen in the employ of the English East India Company were forced to flee. The Englishmen, arriving in Siam were well received by King Narai, and reported to their superiors of prevailing conditions in Siam. By 1661 the English East India Company was once again in business in Siam: Thomas Cotes being placed in charge of the English factory at Ayudhya.[24]

The British presence in Siam at once aroused the hostility of the Dutch—a presence in no small measure responsible for the aggressive war which the latter waged against the Siamese kingdom in 1664. The Dutch wanted no competition in gathering the wealth of Siam.[25] The English, although in business again, were not very successful in drumming wealth into their coffers and were much plagued by interlopers.* Many of the English interlopers were in the service of the king of Siam and received his protection, a fact which embarrassed the English company and strained its relations with the Kingdom of Siam.

The French, heretofore an unknown factor in eastern parts, commenced in the second half of the seventeenth century a vigorous expansion in the orient. Although lacking the commercial instincts of the Dutch, the French made strenuous efforts to acquire influence at the court of Ayudhya. French interest in the far east found expression in the *Société des Missions Etrangères*, established in Paris in 1659 to proselytize in the orient independently of the Jesuits. The new society, supported by King Louis XIV (1643-1715), was vigorously opposed not only by Jesuits (the pioneers in eastern missionary activity), but by the Portuguese and Spanish as well who divined the intent of Louis XIV to spread French influence in the far east.

En route for Vietnam, Bishop Lambert de la Motte landed at Mergui in April 1662. The French bishop visited Ayudhya before embarking for Vietnam in a vessel which was wrecked. The luckless bishop, returning to the Siamese capital, was joined by a second prelate, Bishop Pallu, and four priests in January 1664. Severe persecution of the Catholic population in Vietnam induced the missionaries to remain in Siam. King Narai treated the proselytizers well, manifesting his friendship by allowing the missionaries to build a church and seminary. Bishops Lambert de la Motte and Pallu, therefore, decided to establish the headquarters of the mission at Ayudhya. The missionaries before long were active, even in the outlying districts of Siam.[26]

Meanwhile events of a significant nature were transpiring to the north. The Southern Ming pretender, Yung-Li (d. 1662), was driven from China in 1658, taking refuge in Burma with seven hundred followers.[27] Chiengmai, in fear of invasion by supporters of the Mings who were ravaging northern Burma, requested Ayudhyan aid, but in 1660 when King Narai marched northward with

---

* In the present context Englishmen who traded in the east without the sanction of the English East India Company thereby infringing the trade monopoly granted the company by the British crown.

a large army he found Chiengmai no longer solicitous for his assistance, and the king of Ayudhya was obliged to retire.[28] The Burmese, purposing to repel Ming attacks on Ava summoned Mon levies in defense of the city.   A revolt at Martaban ca. 1661 revealed the extent of Mon discontent in Lower Burma. Thousands of Mons, in apprehension of Burmese reprisals, fled to Thailand.[29] The Burmese pursued the refugees by the Ataran River and the Three Pagodas Pass into Siam,[30] but were defeated by the Siamese at Kanburi.[31] In 1662 the Siamese raided deep into Burma, but their interest was focused primarily on Chiengmai which they captured in the same year.[32] The Ayudhyans in the Chiengmai campaign were commanded by the P'ya Kosa T'ibodi—a severe disciplinarian.[33] The Burmese were powerless to intervene since King Pye (1661-72) was threatened by the Manchus, the new ruling dynasty in China.   Nevertheless the people of Chiengmai still maintained a spark of the old spirit of independence.   In 1664 they rose in revolt against the Ayudhyans, and drove the southern Thai from the principality.   A Burmese prince was reinstated as a vassal of the court of Ava.   Chiengmai remained tied to its Burmese suzerain until 1727.[34] In the only other war with an Asian neighbor, the Siamese in 1679 successfully intervened in a Cambodian succession dispute placing their candidate on the throne of the ancient Khmers.   The Thai invasion of Cambodia is mentioned in Cambodian but not Siamese history.[35]

The favor shown to the English and French rankled with the Dutch who demanded concessions favorable to their well nurtured commercial interests. The Siamese balked, and the Dutch blockaded the mouth of the Menam River. King Narai, unable to counter the Dutch naval pressure, swallowed his pride humbling his kingdom on the altar of Dutch avarice by concluding a humiliating treaty with the Hollanders in August of 1664.   The treaty granted the Dutch a monopoly of the commerce of hides and a virtual monopoly of Thailand's seaborne commerce with China.[36] By terms of the treaty * the Siamese agreed not to employ Chinese seamen (the dominant personnel of the Siamese merchant marine) on Thai ships plying the China trade.   The Dutch, therefore, rendered it virtually impossible for Thai ships to compete successfully with their own vessels in the trade with China [37] since the Siamese are not noted seamen.   The Dutch also obtained certain extraterritorial privileges of jurisdiction in Siam;[38] the beginning of a system which in the nineteenth century placed the Thais in a position of inferiority in the adjudication of disputes between Thai nationals and foreigners.

Following the Dutch blockade of the Menam River, King Narai cogitated measures to prevent a recurrence of the salient lesson in the application of naval power.   About this time Father Thomas Valguarnera, an Italian with the French missionaries, assisted the Thai king in his distress by designing and superintending the construction of forts at Ayudhya, Bangkok and Nonthaburi against future Dutch aggression.   King Narai even moved his residence, but apparently not the capital, to Lopburi where a new palace and defensive works were constructed with the assistance of Father Thomas.[39]

The Catholic missionaries established in Thailand were not the only foreign religionists seeking to acquire a foothold in the country.   In 1668 Mohammedan

---

* For the text of the treaty see Appendix III.

activists arrived in Siam from Acheen (Acheh), and sought to convert King Narai to the religion of the Prophet but with no success. The king in fact at a later date declared if he changed religion he would never embrace Mohammedanism, a consolation of a sort to Christian missionaries who found King Narai equally intractable about embracing the tenets of Christianity.[40] The French missionaries, notwithstanding the lack of success in converting King Narai personally, were not long in sending over-optimistic reports to France of proselytizing success in the Kingdom of Siam. The court of Versailles conceived the idea that the conversion of Siam was now in the offing.[41] In May 1673, Pallu, the Bishop of Heliopolis, returned to Siam after a stay abroad with letters from King Louis XIV and the Pope to King Narai. Bishop Pallu protested against appearing at court in stocking feet and prostrating before the king in accordance with Siamese usage. Protocol was waived. The Thai nobles, however, were scandalized when the bishops and priests remained seated during the royal audience at which the letters were presented to the king.[42]

The letter of Louis XIV was so well received by King Narai that Bishops Pallu and Lambert de la Motte pressed the king to dispatch an embassy to France. King Narai had not previously given serious attention to an alliance with France, against Holland, but the dangerous extension of Dutch influence in the Kingdom of Siam, signalized by the unequal treaty of 1664, no doubt induced the king to view favorably a league with King Louis XIV—the greatest European monarch of the age. France and the Netherlands were at war in Europe. The projected Thai-French alliance, however, "hung fire" for a number of years.[43]

While French-Ayudhyan relations suffered from the vagaries of an uncertain relationship, French influence in Siam was waxing. By 1676 the Catholic seminary at Ayudhya had enrolled over one hundred pupils, and a female community, the Votaries of the Cross, had been created,[44] testifying to a propagation of the new religion, which if not a spectacular success, had at least broken ground on alien soil.

The British, meanwhile, were not as adept as the French and Dutch at winning friends or influencing the Siamese. In 1678 the Bantam * council of the English East India Company commissioned Richard Burnaby to investigate the causes of the flagging trade at the Ayudhya factory. With Burnaby traveled Constantine Phaulkon, a Greek by birth, who had entered the service of the English East India Company, had won a reward for saving the magazine at Bantam, and then resigned to try his fortune in Siam. Phaulkon, as we shall see, became a dominating figure in seventeenth century Siam.[45]

Constantine Phaulkon, an innkeeper's son, was born on the island of Cephalonia.** The future royal adviser and virtual prime minister of Siam, absconded from home to become a cabin boy on a British merchant ship. In 1680 Richard Burnaby and George White (an interloper who had recently entered the service of the English East India Company), proposed to augment British influence at the court of Ayudhya by having Phaulkon enter the service of Siam and use his influence to obtain concessions for English trading interests. Phaulkon, in execution of the plan, found work as an interpreter, the employee of

---

* A city on the island of Java
** Off the west coast of Greece

British subjects found there to leave Siam. The ships conveying the proclamation of King James II reached Mergui in June 1687. The English at the seaport manifested an intention to comply with the order of James II. However Anthony Weltden, the leader of the British expedition, with unsuspecting levity, joined the English on the shore in lavish entertainments oblivious to danger of a Siamese attack. On the night of July 14th (O.S.) Siamese artillery opened fire on the British ships, sinking the *James* while the Siamese massacred most of the English on shore. Weltden was among the few surviving Englishmen to escape with his life. As a consequence of Weltden's action at Mergui Siam officially declared war against the English East India Company in August 1687—one month before the arrival of Desfarges's expedition.[62] The Siamese declaration of war, however, remained virtually a nullity as neither side took steps to inflict a real defeat on the other. No formal peace was declared and the war died a natural death.[63]

While the British in the Kingdom of Ayudhya were descending a road strewn with marks of their ineptitude and folly, the French were apparently ascending the path leading to empire, while the wily Dutch, with shrewder instinct held their hand awaiting the inevitable reaction in Siam consequent upon the landing of a large body of foreign troops. The Dutch did not have long to wait.

When in September 1687 the expedition of Desfarges arrived in Siam, Constantine Phaulkon was faced with a dilemma. The French occupation of Bangkok and Mergui was bound to be unpopular with the Siamese and raise suspicion as to the ultimate French intention in Thailand. On the other hand if Phaulkon refused the French demands his plans of co-operation with Louis XIV for the conversion of Siam to Christianity might be ruined. Phaulkon resolved to follow the boldest course, but to soothe the susceptibilities of his royal master and the Thais, Phaulkon exacted an oath of allegiance from Desfarges and his soldiers in favor of the king of Siam, insisting that the French troops become mercenaries in the Thai service. Desfarges was then allowed to occupy Bangkok, which he strongly fortified, while du Bruant was commissioned to command at Mergui with a garrison of one hundred and twenty men. In time two plenipotentiaries of France were able to conclude a treaty granting the subjects of the French king permission to build trading establishments, extraterritorial jurisdiction over French subjects within the realm of Siam and the cession of all islands within a radius of ten miles of Mergui.[64]

As Phaulkon's meteoric star was being attached to the tail of the French comet now sweeping into Siam, the Greek adventurer adopted an uncompromising stand toward the Dutch. The Dutch position became untenable, and in 1686 their factory was shut down. With the closing of the Dutch factory the *raison d'être* of the French expedition lapsed. The smallness of the force under the command of Desfarges and its wide dispersal prevented an effective counter in case of serious Thai disaffection, which in the circumstances was all but inevitable.[65]

> "To make matters worse [for the French], Phaulkon in supporting the demands of the Jesuits quarrelled hopelessly with Bishop Laneau, the head of the Missions Etrangères at Ayut'ia, and a serious rift appeared in the French camp. Then in

March 1688 King Narai became so seriously ill [with dropsy] at Lopburi that he was unable to conduct business. This gave an opportunity for an anti-foreign conspiracy led by Pra P'etraja, the general in charge of the royal elephants, to gain control over the palace. Too late Phaulkon summoned Desfarges to his aid; thousands of armed Siamese were rallying to the cause of the conspirators. Pra P'etraja was appointed regent, and in the middle of May he arrested Phaulkon. The French, threatened by overwhelming numbers of Siamese troops, were thrown upon the defensive and could do nothing to save their ally. On July 5 he was publicly executed. In the next month [July 11th according to others] the king died and Pra P'etraja was raised to the throne." [66]

While the Siamese revolution of 1688 was transpiring a Thai embassy arrived in Europe July 1688 after eight months at sea. The embassy journeyed to Rome arriving on December 20, 1688 (N.S.). The Thai ambassadors were received in audience by Pope Innocent XI (1676-89) on the 23rd, and a letter of King Narai was presented to and read by the Pope.[67]

MESSAGE OF KING NARAI TO POPE INNOCENT XI

"The King of Ayudhya to His Holiness Innocent XI, Supreme Pontiff of the Holy See,

Greetings:

"Since we have ascended the Throne of Ayudhya, it has been Our wish to cultivate acquaintances with the great Sovereigns of Europe and to exchange with them correspondence in order to foster mutual friendship, which We hope might be the means of introducing into Our country the benefits of western knowledge, thereby giving enlightenment to Our people. While thus pondering and before we sent over an embassy with that object in view, Your Holiness anticipated Us by deputing the Bishop of Heliopolis to Us with Your gracious letter and presents, which We have received with great pleasure. We therefore send [sent] an embassy bearing Our letter and presents to reciprocate Your Holiness' expression of friendship and to strengthen the more the bonds thereof so that the two nations may be cemented as one golden land united and indivisible. To Our regret, however, Our embassy never succeeded in reaching its high destination, having been shipwrecked off the Cape of Good Hope and all Our presents scattered on the high seas.

"We have therefore again despatched another embassy bearing Our complimentary letter and presents and have attached thereto the Reverend Tachard to act in a guiding capacity. By sending this mission We hope to give yet another testimonial of Our constant purpose to support the Christian missionaries who have come to spread their Religion in this country as well as people who have embraced it. We would take this opportunity to assure Your Holiness that it shall be Our duty to look after them in such a manner that You shall not need be anxious of their welfare. For this purpose We have instructed Father Tachard to inform Your Holiness in Our name of all that You may wish to know. May Your Holiness accept the presents We have much pleasure in sending in order to strengthen the bonds of friendship existing between Your Holiness and Ourselves.

"May the Supreme Power in the Universe grant Your Holiness a long life for the benefit of Your Religion. May it spread gloriously throughout the world." [68]

From Your Holiness' true friend.
(royal seal)

(countersigned) Phaulkon

The presents brought for the Pope included a golden box engraved by Thai goldsmiths, a gift of King Narai, and a silver box carved in the Japanese fashion, on a silver tray, a present of Constantine Phaulkon. The Thai ambassadors of whom Okkhun Chamnan seems to be the only ambassador known by name, paid their reverences to the Pope and then withdrew.[69]

Pope Innocent XI reciprocated the Thai expressions of good will by entrusting Father Tachard with return presents including a telescope. "This will be highly appreciated by the King who is interested in beholding the astonishing operations of the Mathematical sciences which the Fathers, going to his Royal Palace, often explain to him." Gifts were bestowed on members of the embassy, and the "First Minister" (Phaulkon) was presented, in absentia, with a Monte crystal box, embellished with silver ornaments, and a painting of the Virgin Mary with the child Jesus—the work of the artist Maratta. In addition letters were written to Constantine Phaulkon and to King Narai, both of whom unbeknown to Pope Innocent XI had passed into eternity.[70] We conclude the present chapter with the letter to King Narai:

LETTER OF POPE INNOCENT XI TO KING NARAI

Dated Rome, 7th January 1689 (N.S.)

"Illustrious and most Puissant King, health and light of Divine Grace be unto you.

"The coming of Our beloved Son, Father Tachard, of the Society of Jesus, has been more agreeable to Us than We can express. Your Majesty, doubtful of the success of the first Embassy, sent Us this Father as Delegate Extraordinary. From Your Majesty's royal letters, which the same father handed to Us, and from those things which he most eloquently expressed to Us viva voce in Your Name, We have been made aware to our boundless exaltation that you foster a most well-inclined will towards the faithful of Christ and that you are predisposed, not only in favour of the Fathers of the above-mentioned Society, but also towards all those who profess the Christian religion in your dominions and in other regions of the Far East, to protect them with your royal patronage and

67

to help them with generous liberality when they have recourse to Your Majesty. Now, as the propagation of this religion is the principal care of Our pastoral solicitude, We cannot sufficiently testify by words Our superabounding joy when We consider the increase that this same religion will obtain by leaning upon Your Majesty's assistance. And in reciprocation, We wish Your Majesty to be fully persuaded that We will not neglect any opportunity to declare the high degree of esteem in which We hold Your Majesty; and that above all We will not omit to pray, unfailingly and earnestly, that Sun which knows no setting, that he may pour down on Your Majesty the rays of His light and openly show you the way which leads to life.

"The above mentioned Father Tachard, a man distinguished for piety and virtue, and whom, therefore, We entrust to You with earnest entreaty, will closely show Your Majesty the feelings of Our soul, and will at the same time express to You the proofs of the benevolence We bear Your Royal Person. It remains that Your Majesty fulfil Our expectations whilst We eagerly call down upon Your Majesty from Almighty God all prosperity.

"Given at Rome, near St. Mary Major, under the seal of the Fisherman's Ring, the 7th day of January, 1689, in the XIII year of our Pontificate." [71]

BIBLIOGRAPHY

1. Anderson, John. *English Intercourse with Siam in the Seventeenth Century*, Kegan Paul, Trench & Co., Ltd., London, 1890.

2. Busch, Noel F. *Thailand*, D. Van Nostrand Company, Inc., Princeton, New Jersey, 1964.

3. Carretto, P. "Vatican Papers of the XVII Century," *Journal of the Siam Society*, Vol. VII, Bangkok, 1959.

4. Giles, Francis H. "A Critical Analysis of Van Vliet's Historical Account of Siam in the 17th Century," *Journal of the Siam Society*, Vol. VII, Bangkok, 1959.

5. Hall, D. G. E. *A History of South-East Asia*, MacMillan & Co., Ltd., London, and St. Martin's Press, New York, 1961.

6. Hutchinson, E. W. "Four French State Manuscripts," *Journal of the Siam Society*, Vol. VIII, Bangkok, 1959.

7. "Intercourse between Burma and Siam, as recorded in Hmannan Yazawindawgyi," *Journal of the Siam Society*, Vol. V, Part 1, Bangkok, 1959.

8. *Records of the Relations between Siam and Foreign Countries in the 17th Century*, Printed by order of the Council of the Vajiranana National Library, Vol. II, Bangkok, 1916, and Vol. V, Bangkok, 1921.

9. Wood, W. A. R. *A History of Siam*, The Siam Barnakich Press, Bangkok, 1933.

FOOTNOTES

1. Wood, 176.
2. Ibid., 177-80. Giles, relying on statements by the contemporary van Vliet, states peace was effected by the mediation of the king of Queda (Kedah); See Giles, 134. Wood does not give his source.
3. Records, etc., Vol. II, 1.
4. Wood, 180, 181.
5. Ibid., 181, 182.
6. Ibid., 182. Hall wrongly ascribes the Dutch altercation with Siam to the year 1649. Van Vliet, mentioned by Hall specifically, was not Dutch factor at Ayudhya in 1649 as he implies; See Hall, 301. Van Vliet, however, was the Dutch factor at Ayudhya for the period 1636-41, and therefore was positioned to defend the interests of Dutch commerce in Siam during 1639.
7. Wood, 182, 183.
8. Records, etc., Vol. II, 6.
9. Wood, 183.
10. Records, etc., Vol. II, 7.
11. Ibid., 10, 11.
12. Wood, 183, 184.
13. Records, etc., Vol. II, 16.
14. Ibid., 19.
15. Wood, 201.
16. Ibid., 186, 187.
17. Ibid., 187.
18. Records, etc., Vol. II, 20.
19. Wood, 187, 188.
20. Ibid., 189. The *P'ongsawadan* states that Chao Fa Jai was appointed to the kingship by his father; See Wood, 189.
21. Wood, 189.
22. Ibid., 189, 190.
23. Ibid., 190.
24. Ibid., 190, 191; Records, etc., Vol. II, 22-30.
25. Anderson, 97.
26. Hall, 302, 303.
27. Ibid., 320.
28. Ibid., 302.
29. Ibid., 320.
30. Ibid., 302.
31. Ibid., 320; Consult the *Hmannan Yazawin Dawgyi* for a somewhat different version of this war.
32. Hall, 302.
33. Wood, 192.
34. Hall, 302. The Burmese chronicle, the *Hmannan Yazawin Dawgyi*, indicates that the king of Burma appointed Minye Hlakyaw to the governorship of Chiengmai. He left for Chiengmai in December 1664, after the Siamese were driven from Zinme (Chiengmai) by its people. About the year 1667, Minye Hlakyaw was accused of disloyalty and was replaced by the Sawbwa of Mohnyin. Four years later ca. 1671 a certain Minye Yanta was appointed

governor of Chiengmai; See "Intercourse, etc.," 180, 181.

35. Wood, 212.
36. Hall, 303; Consult my Appendix III.
37. Wood, 195; Consult my Appendix III.
38. Hall, 303; Consult my Appendix III.
39. Wood, 195, 196.
40. Ibid., 196, 197.
41. Hall, 303.
42. Wood, 197, 198.
43. Hall, 303, 304.
44. Wood, 197.
45. Hall, 304.
46. Ibid.
47. Ibid., 304, 305.
48. Ibid., 305.
49. Wood, 199; Consult Records, etc., Vol. III.
50. Hall, 305, 306.
51. Ibid., 306.
52. Wood, 200.
53. Hutchinson, 109, 110.
54. Hall, 306.
55. Ibid., 306, 307.
56. Wood, 205.
57. Hall, 307, 308.
58. Busch, 56-58.
59. Wood, 201.
60. Ibid., 205-07; Consult Records, etc., Vol. IV.
61. Wood, 207; Consult Records, etc., Vol. IV.
62. Hall, 310, 311; Records, etc., Vol. V, 7, 8.
63. Hall, 314.
64. Ibid., 308, 309; Consult also my Appendix IV.
65. Hall, 311.
66. Ibid., 312. A Portuguese report states the king was poisoned by P'etraja; See Records, etc., Vol. V, 56.
67. Carretto, 178, 179.
68. Ibid., 180, 181.
69. Ibid., 178, 179.
70. Ibid., 187, 188.
71. Ibid., 189, 190.

THE LATE AYUDHYA PERIOD 1629 - 1767 — PART 2
UNTIL THE ABDICATION OF KING UT'UMP'ON IN 1758

I. P'ETRAJA 1688-1703

King P'etraja ascended the throne of Ayudhya with a French garrison at Bangkok—pitted in the breast of his kingdom—an immediate threat to his own security as well as the continued independence of Siam.   P'etraja, shortly before the death of King Narai, had invited the French commander, Desfarges, to conduct his French troops to Lopburi many miles in the interior of the country.[1] The following extract explains the Siamese motive:

EXTRACT OF A LETTER FROM P'YA KOSA T'IBODI (KOSA PAN), FORMER SIAMESE AMBASSADOR TO FRANCE, TO MR. MARTIN, GOVERNOR OF PONDICHERRY, AMONG OTHERS

Dated, 27th December 1693 (presumably N.S.)

"It was decided thereupon to entice the General up to Lopburi.   He, having heard nothing of Phaulkon's arrest made no difficulty about coming.   The motive for our confidential treatment of him was to prevent the French from spreading the alarm, since we feared that du Bruant and de Beauregard [French commanders at Mergui], who were in Phaulkon's confidence, might take fright and commit some unfriendly action.

"We therefore represented that we had news from the North of impending trouble, which made it necessary that his troops with du Bruant's should effect a junction with the Siamese army at a given spot—the army to be despatched to stem the enemy's advance." * [2]

Desfarges, apparently learning of the death of Phaulkon, temporized, persuading the Siamese that his presence with his officers at Bangkok was necessary to enforce compliance with Siamese orders.** [3]   Desfarges portraying the obstinacy of two officers, offered personally to fetch them, leaving his two sons, among others, as hostages at Lopburi.[4]

CONTINUATION OF THE EXTRACT OF THE LETTER OF P'YA KOSA T'IBODI

"We do not know what decision he came to with his staff after leaving Lopburi.   We do know however that the French Officers arrested their Siamese and Portuguese colleagues, opened fire and, burnt the General's quarters near the Fort, blew up 13 cannon in the West Fort, spiking the re-

---

* In the interior of the country, the small force of Desfarges, deprived of the protection of the fort at Bangkok, would be wholly (or unholy) at the mercy of larger Siamese forces.

** The reader will recall that Phaulkon exacted an oath of allegiance from Desfarges in favor of the king of Siam.

mainder which they were unable to destroy, and transferring the arms and ammunition to the fort on the opposite side of the river.

"The Siamese immediately invaded the abandoned fort. Desfarges seeing them, ordered his men to re-take it; but they, after fighting for some time, were compelled to withdraw to their fort on the east side of the river, and then proceeded to do much damage." [5]

The Siamese laid siege to the French fortress at Bangkok. A French junior officer, St. Cricq, attempted to establish liaison with French ships known to be patrolling in the Gulf of Siam. St. Cricq, proceeding downstream from Bangkok by boat, was surrounded by numerous Thai craft, and the Frenchman perceiving no chance of escape, allowed the Ayudhyans to close. St. Cricq then fired the powder magazine—destroying many Siamese adversaries, as well as forfeiting his own life in the process.[6]

The siege of Bangkok, conducted at first with vigor by the Siamese, languished as the summer advanced.

"Desfarges attributed the change in their [the Siamese] demeanour to the impression made upon them by St. Cricq's desperate action. Kosa Pan claimed afterwards that the French asked for terms. Probably what happened was that the French Jesuits in the Fort succeeded in communicating with Bishop Laneau, whom the Siamese employed as their intermediary, and that through these channels the Siamese learnt that Desfarges was prepared to withdraw from the country on terms." [7]

In September 1688, after the death of King Narai, an accord was reached with the French who were allowed to evacuate Siam with the honors of war, taking with them cannon, munitions and baggage while returning the fortress at Bangkok intact to the Siamese. The Jesuits were allowed to remain in the kingdom in the enjoyment of the conferments proffered by the late King Narai while the French East India Company retained concessions granted previously. Hostages were exchanged on both sides. In November of 1688 the French evacuated Bangkok.[8] Previous to the departure of the French Bangkok force du Bruant and de Beauregard burst out of Mergui, taking with them sixteen cannon and fifty rifles embarking in a Siamese ship and a British vessel seized in the harbor.[9] The failure of Desfarges to release his hostages, shortly after the French hostages held by the Siamese were allowed to board Desfarges's boat, incensed the Siamese.

"The Siamese highly enraged at the loss of their hostages, stirred up a sanguinary persecution, and the Bishop of Metallopolis was the first to suffer. He was taken off his ship and dragged in the mire with every possible insult, exposed for a long time to heat of the sun and to torments of insects. Some pulled him by the beard, others spat in his face and those who could not get near enough to strike, threw mud at him." [10]

Other Frenchmen were treated to similar indignities and many lost their lives.[11]

flogged to death had not the aged Chief Queen of King P'etraja interceded for them." * [33]

A gate at the palace of King P'rachao Sua acquired the name "Gate of Corpses" because the bodies of murdered children were carried through the gate: victims of lust and cruelty—a monument to the ferocity of "King Tiger." [34]

King P'rachao Sua being:

"... a prey to superstition and debauchery, surrendered himself entirely to the idolatrous priests, who, by their austerities, engaged to expiate his faults. Following his example, everyone built temples. Trade and manufactures languished and the populace given up to fantastic ceremonies no longer gave thought to the question of the defences of the State. The false gods had many worshippers and the State had no soldiers available for defence. Fortune favoured the kingdom as the neighbouring Kings were all engaged in war against each other and having too much on their hands at home, had no time to think of foreign aggression." [35]

In addition to the scourges of a vicious king, the Siamese in the early eighteenth century labored under penalties imposed by nature as the kingdom was visited by a severe drought and famine. The fertile soil was transformed to dust while the rice crop was dangerously depleted. "The water of the [Menam] River naturally clear and limpid, suddenly became green and turbid." A green scum covered the waters of the great river. After fifteen days, however, the phenomenon disappeared. The rains fell, and the land once again regained its wonted fertility. [36]

The Dutch, who remained the dominant European interest at Ayudhya, during the eighteenth century, had a difficult time securing their mercantile interests. Gideon Tant, Chief Factor at Ayudhya, in a report dated March 1705, laments the difficulty of purchasing sappanwood and tin. The sale of imported cloth to the Siamese was also difficult. Treaties were not adhered to by the Ayudhyans, and by the end of 1705 the Dutch factories at Ayudhya and Ligor were temporarily shut down but only until the following year. The Dutch in the years that followed operated their establishments in Siam at a considerable loss, but the Dutchmen were afraid to withdraw from the Siam trade lest a European power outbid their influence at the court of Ayudhya. [37]

King P'rachao Sua died in 1709; agewise in his middle forties, worn-out by drunkenness and debauchery; the term of the infamous reign of a tyrant of few attainments and those of an evil nature. [38]

III. PU'MINT'ARAJA OR T'AI SRA 1709-33

King Pu'mint'araja, the eldest son of P'rachao Sua, succeeded to the throne of Ayudhya at the age of twenty-eight without opposition. The younger brother of the new king, Prince Bant'un Noi, was appointed to the office of Maha Uparat. [39] The principal events of the reign of King Pu'mint'araja relate to a

---

* His Excellency, Sukich Nimmanheminda, the Thai Ambassador to the United States, informs me the mother of Kosa Pan is the proper instrument of intercession for the sons of P'rachao Sua, not the Chief Queen of P'etraja, as asserted by Wood in this quotation.

succession dispute in Cambodia and the subsequent war involving not only the contending parties in Cambodia but also Siam and the Nguyen of Hue.

In 1714 Prea Srey Thomea (called Sri T'ammaraja by the Siamese), the king of Cambodia, was toppled from his throne by Keo Fa with the assistance of Vietnamese troops. Prea Srey Thomea and his younger brother fled to Ayudhya. King Pu'mint'araja espoused the cause of Prea Srey Thomea, but efforts to restore the fallen king to his throne failed both in 1715 and in 1716.[40]

Finally in 1717 two Siamese armies advanced on Cambodia. The northern army, led by P'ya Chakri, advanced by Siem Reap, north of the Tonle Sap. A smaller army, supported by a large fleet, advanced along the coast of Cambodia. The P'rak'lang, a man of Chinese extract, led the southern forces. The P'rak'lang was both incompetent and cowardly,[41] although, he at least, was cognizant of his deficiencies, accepting the charge with reluctance. King Pu'mint'araja, however, would not be gainsaid, as related by the contemporary Briton, Alexander Hamilton, in *A New Account of the East Indies*,* first published in 1727.

> "In Anno 1717. the King of Siam made War on his Neighbour of Cambodia, and invaded his Country with an Army of 50000 by Land, and 20000 by Sea, and committed the Care of his Armies to his Barkalong [**], a Chinese, altogether unacquainted with War. The China Man accepted of the Charge with much Reluctancy, but the King would not be denied." [42]

Hamilton was not aware of the progress of the northern army under P'ya Chakri as no mention of engagements of greater consequence appears in the vivid description, by Hamilton, of the disasters which overtook the southern force commanded by the P'rak'lang.

> "When the Siam Army and Fleet threatened Cambodia, the King knew his Inability to withstand the Siamers, so the Inhabitants that lived on his Borders had Orders to remove towards the City of Cambodia [Oudong?], and what they could not bring with them, to destroy it, so that for fifty Leagues the Country was a mere Desert. He then addrest the King of Couchin-china for Assistance and Protection, which he obtained, on Condition, that Cambodia should become tributary to Couchin-china, which was agreed to, and he had an Army of 15000 to assist him by Land, and 3000 in nimble Gallies well mann'd and equipt, by Sea.
>
> "The Siam Army by Land was above double in Number of the Cambodians and Couchin-chinese in Conjunction, and their Fleet above four Times their Number. The Land Army finding all the Country desolate, as they marched into the

---

* The observations and remarks of Captain Hamilton relate to the years 1688-1723—a period in which he traveled and traded between the Cape of Good Hope and Japan.

** The P'rak'lang or the Minister of the Treasury—who by the eighteenth century had assumed the burdens of a number of functions unrelated to his original office.

Borders of Cambodia, soon began to be in Distress for Want of Provisions, which obliged them to kill their Carriage Beasts, and their Elephants and Horses which they could get no Sustenance for, and the Soldiers being obliged to eat their Flesh, it being a Diet they had never been used to, an epidemick Flux and Fever seized the whole Army, so that in two Months one half was not left, and those were obliged to retreat towards their own Country again, with the Cambodian Army always at their Heels.

"Nor had their Navy much better Success, for they coming to Ponteamass [the Hatien of today], sent in their small Gallies to plunder and burn the Town, which they did effectually, and, of Elephants' Teeth only, they burnt above 200 Tuns. The Ships and Jonks of Burden lying, in the Road, above four Miles from the Town, the Couchin-chinese taking hold of the Opportunity, attackt the large Vessels, and burnt some, and forced others ashore, whilst their Gallies were in a narrow River, and could not come to their Assistance till High-water that they could get out. The Couchin-chinese having done what they came for, retired, not caring to engage such a superior Number, and the Siamers fearing Famine in their Fleet, steered their Course for Siam with Disgrace. In Anno 1720. I saw several of the Wracks, and the Ruins of the Town of Pontcamass." [43]

Wood states the Siamese army was attacked and defeated at Banteay M'eas (Hatien) by the combined forces of the enemy. The defeat of the southern army, precipitated by a panic of the naval force, resulted in a disorderly retreat in which the Ayudhyans lost many men and all their artillery.[44]

The northern army, commanded by P'ya Chakri, redeemed Thai arms, but the avowed object of the campaign, namely the restoration of Prea Srey Thomea (Sri T'ammaraja), was not realized, in the circumstances, redounding to the discredit of King Pu'mint'araja. Nevertheless the war against Cambodia must be reckoned a success for reasons of state, as follows, since the Cambodians once again recognized Siamese suzerainty—

The army of P'ya Chakri defeated the Cambodians in several engagements, skirting the northern edge of the Tonle Sap, and then advanced to Oudong, at that time the capital of the country. Keo Fa, faced with immediate deposition and perhaps a worse fate, offered to do homage for his kingdom, sending the standard gold and silver trees in token of his submission to King Pu'mint'araja. The Thais deeming such obeisance sufficient, resolved to leave King Keo Fa in peaceful possession of his throne to rule as a tributary of the Kingdom of Siam.[45] The former king of Cambodia, Prea Srey Thomea, undoubtedly viewed peace as an unnecessary blessing at the present juncture, especially when his patrons, or former patrons, were poised to set the ex-king once again on his throne.

Following the termination of the Ayudhyan-Cambodian war events not unworthy of our attention transpired at Chiengmai. During 1727 the people of Zinme (Chiengmai) revolted against the rule of the Burmese, who the reader will recall maintained the suzerainty of Chiengmai from the year 1626, except

79

for a brief period in the early 1660s. Many Burmese were massacred including the Burman prince of Chiengmai. A certain Kanan Deikba was elected prince of Chiengmai (apparently the T'ep Singh of Wood). The Burmese, responding quickly to the affront of outraged majesty, dispatched an expedition of fifty elephants, two thousand horse and twenty thousand men via Mone (Muang Nai) in October 1727 to suppress the rebellion. The Burmese were commanded by Minye Yandathu. The city of Chiengmai was recaptured, but the Burmese officers, accepting a light view of their charge, were bribed to evacuate the city. In 1731 the Burmese once again attempted to bring Zinme (Chiengmai) under subjugation, but were defeated in battle by the northern Thai. Until 1763 Chiengmai, though disturbed by internecine convulsions, maintained a precarious independence: the twilight of her independent existence.[46]

The reign of King Pu'mint'araja, on the whole, was a peaceful passage in time. The king completed a canal (the Mahajai) commenced by his father, and repaired or built a number of temples in the land. However, the hydra of future strife raised a head when King Pu'mint'araja sought to change the order of succession from Prince Bant'un Noi, the younger brother of the king (appointed Maha Uparat) to Prince Naren, the eldest son. Prince Naren conceived the alteration of the succession to the crown an act of injustice, and retired, shortly afterward, to a monastery. King Pu'mint'araja, either because of a deep-seated aversion toward the Uparat, or perhaps more naturally for reasons of parental affection, did not abate his wish to alter the succession. When King Pu'mint'araja was taken ill, the king, realizing that death could not be denied, proclaimed Prince Ap'ai, his second son, as the heir to the throne. The Maha Uparat and Prince Ap'ai were preparing to resolve their respective claims by resort to arms when King Pu'mint'araja died in January 1733 at the age of fifty-four.[47]

> "King T'ai Sra [Pu'mint'araja] is spoken of by Siamese historians as a cruel and sinful man, mainly, it would seem, on the ground that he was extremely fond of hunting and fishing. He does not, however, appear to have been hard or unmerciful to his subjects, and he cannot be regarded as a bad or unsuccessful ruler. The worst error of his life was made when he was dying, for his unjust attempt to alter the succession was the cause of much bloodshed and misery."[48]

IV. MAHA T'AMMARAJA II OR BOROMOKOT 1733-58

A violent succession dispute immediately convulsed the Kingdom of Ayudhya when the breath of life departed the body of Pu'mint'araja. Prince Ap'ai collected forty thousand adherents at the Royal Palace. His purse was secure by his control of the treasury. The followers of Prince Ap'ai included among others the P'ya Chakri (Prime Minister) and the P'ya P'rak'lang (Minister of the Treasury).[49] The French contemporary Turpin declares:

> "The union of the nobility under the flag of the young Prince, seemed to indicate that his cause would be successful, but in reality it was the cause of his downfall, owing to internal jealousies as to who should be leader. The higher officials thought that the Barcalon[*] misusing his almost un-

---

* The aggressive tendencies of the Barcalon (P'rak'lang) lead us to believe the inept Barcalon, who bungled the Cambodian invasion, was no longer at the head of his department.

limited power, wished to use them as tools for his personal aggrandisement.

"They appeared to fear that having been sufficiently powerful to hold the Crown Prince [Maha Uparat] in subjection, he would yield to the temptation of taking the crown for himself.

"It seemed more fit that they should obey their old masters rather than to see themselves reduced to ask favours of an equal, and thus all plotted secretly to destroy their work." [50]

The Maha Uparat could rally only five thousand liegemen to support his cause, but the party of the Uparat was united in purpose, a supreme advantage, and enjoyed the support of the people of Ayudhya.[51]

Shots were exchanged between the Royal Palace and the Palace of the Maha Uparat. The P'rak'lang, taking the bull by the horns, advanced with forces toward the Palace of the Maha Uparat, routing the forces of the Uparat in hand to hand combat, and pursuing the foe to the walls of the palace. The P'rak'lang wished to capture the palace by immediate assault, but influenced by members of his entourage more hesitant, the minister deferring to their wishes, postponed the attack (the onset of evening was imminent) until the following day. Thus the forces pledged to support Prince Ap'ai, by their failure to press the advantage which victory had given them, lost the initiative, allowing the enemy time to bind his wounds, sort his forces and plan a future course of action. The Maha Uparat, informed by spies of the dispositions—both physical and moral—within the camp of the P'rak'lang prepared to counterattack. A sortie from behind the walls of the beleaguered palace, caught the besiegers by surprise. The sometime supporters of Prince Ap'ai were routed, some being slaughtered with ease while others were scattered like chaff before the wind.[52]

The Maha Uparat pursued the flying foe to the Royal Palace, no doubt, breathing vengeance all the way. The unreliable soldiery of Prince Ap'ai renounced their allegiance without further ado, deserting to the cause of the Maha Uparat—a cause carrying all before it, in the tempest sweeping Ayudhya. P'ya P'rak'lang and P'ya Chakri witnessing the debacle, on high, as they stood upon the walls of the Royal Palace, deserted the trampled banners of Prince Ap'ai under the pretense of sallying forth to issue orders.[53]

Prince Ap'ai, deserted on every side, fled with his younger brother, Prince Borommet.[54] The Uparat—hereafter referred to by his kingly title, Maha T'ammaraja II—seized the Royal Palace. Turpin states Maha T'ammaraja II offered to bestow the crown of Siam on the head of his eldest nephew,* but the religious recluse refused the honor. Perhaps King Maha T'ammaraja II had reason to anticipate a reply in the negative. If so he had nothing to lose by flouting his magnanimity. The character of King Maha T'ammaraja II is best judged in the light of the crimes committed against members of his own family and others. Turpin relates that several princes of the royal family, captured while in the Royal Palace by King Maha T'ammaraja II, were loaded with chains and tortures until death was their only hope.[55]

---

* The Priest-Prince Naren

The two fugitive princes, Ap'ai and Borommet, escaping for the moment the fate which awaited them, hid for a month among the bulrushes, but a servant sent to purchase food was recognized as an adherent of Prince Ap'ai. The secret presence of the princes was wrested from the retainer by torture. Princes Ap'ai and Borommet were apprehended and executed.[56] Such was the fate of the vanquished in the late Ayudhya period: a fate we lament; cruel, perverse and a stigma against the age, but a fate the vanquished themselves often contemplated only to find an incorrigible heart plotting the same with a more supple hand.

P'ya Chakri and P'ya P'rak'lang, two further fugitives of note, had the audacity to appear at Ayudhya in priestly robes seeking to escape the vengeance of King Maha T'ammaraja II under a garment that was respected throughout the kingdom. But in nefarious Ayudhya before the final overthrow by the Burmese in 1767, the most horrendous crimes were not only possible but commonplace. P'ya Chakri and P'ya P'rak'lang were arraigned before a tribunal headed by the chief priest, and subjected to a thorough cross-examination. The judges finding no evidence on which to prosecute the defenders for crimes against the state, King Maha T'ammaraja II sought other methods to encompass their ruin.[57]

> "He took counsel with . . . the legal luminaries of the kingdom, who, after examining the charges on which they had been arraigned, replied, that far from being culpable they were worthy of the highest rewards. The verdict was remarkable, coming from the mouth of judges who trembled under the sceptre of a despot, a single word from whom could degrade or destroy them." [58]

The germ of the old Thai spirit of independence is yet discernible even under the encumbrance of the absolute monarchy, a spirit recast in a mould of adversity fashioned by the hammering blows of a resurgent Burma, a seed which will yet flower on more fruitful soil during the reign of Kings Rama IV (1851-68) and Rama V (1868-1910), culminating in the constitutional monarchy in 1932.

King Maha T'ammaraja II unable to vent his will under the cloak of constitutional means, availed himself of brute force, a crutch on which every despot is able to lean in times of emergency—whether real or imaginary—whether the despot wears the regalia of absolute monarchy, or pretends to popular election. The P'ya Chakri and P'ya P'rak'lang, therefore, were dispatched furtively, in the gloom of night, by five or six Malay dagger wielding henchmen of the obliquitous King Maha T'ammaraja II.[59]

The resentment of King Maha T'ammaraja II against his brother, Pu'mint'-araja was in fact so great he proposed flinging the body of the deceased king in the river. However the king had second thoughts, and abstained from desecrating the dead.[60]

In the same year as the succession dispute (1733), three hundred Chinese of Ayudhya rose in revolt against King Maha T'ammaraja II—apparently a few days after the king secured possession of the Royal Palace and the kingship of Siam. The Chinese attacked the Royal Palace but were repulsed. Forty of the rebels were captured and executed. The Chinese may have been incited by a party favoring the candidacy of Prince Ap'ai to the kingship.[61]

The Chinese merchant trade as well as immigration to Siam had grown steadily throughout the better part of the Ming period (1368-1644) of Chinese history, and although Chinese trade with the Kingdom of Ayudhya declined in the period 1620-32, it expanded once again after the expulsion of the Japanese in 1632.[62] After 1688 and the period of diminishing European influence, the Chinese dominated the foreign trade with the Kingdom of Siam. As for the Dutch, the most successful of the European trading nations during the Ayudhya period, they were unable to engage in profitable trade with the Thai kingdom. The Dutch therefore lost ground to the Chinese in trade competition.

The Chinese were attracted to Thailand because the:

". . . state trading of Kings Prasat Thong, Narai, and their successors provided lucrative employment for [the] Chinese as factors, warehousemen, accountants, and seamen—and without precluding Chinese private trade. As a result of these developments, and in spite of certain restrictions imposed on overseas trade and emigration by the authorities in China, Chinese immigrants were attracted to Siam in ever greater numbers throughout the sixteenth and seventeenth centuries." [63]

Many people of Chinese extraction and culture inhabit Thailand to the present day.

Prince Sena P'itak, the eldest son of King Maha T'ammaraja II, was appointed to the office of Maha Uparat in 1740, although utterly unworthy of the honor, having on one occasion attempted to take the life of the Priest-Prince Naren, for whom King Maha T'ammaraja II had great affection. The king prepared to flog his reprobated son, but Prince Naren interceded on behalf of Prince Sena P'itak, begging the king to pardon the offender. King Maha T'ammaraja II granted the wish of the favorite Naren.[64]

Prince Sena P'itak, however, profited little by the reprieve granted him.

"In April 1756 King Boromokot [King Maha T'ammaraja II] made the discovery that his eldest son, the Maha Uparat, was carrying on an intrigue with two of his own wives. The King's fury passed all bounds, and he gave orders for the Uparat to be scourged two hundred and thirty times. He expired after the one hundred and eightieth stroke. The offending ladies were also flogged to death." [65]

The late Ayudhyan monarchy was approaching the nadir, as well as its term. The sins of Kings Prasat T'ong and P'rachao Sua and others were expiated by the Thai people on the crumbling edifice of the Kingdom of Ayudhya, crushed by the might of Burma in 1767 amid reverberations of a cruel sack of the capital. The Thai people suffered affliction for many years, a prey to invasion from Burma. When the independence of Thailand, wrested from the Burmese in sanguinary combat, had been secured, a new Siam arose on the ruins of the old. In time Bangkok, not Ayudhya, became the capital of a new dynasty, and the center of Thai affairs—a position it has held down to the present day.

The remaining years of the reign of Maha T'ammaraja II shall not detain us long. In 1744 the king of Ayudhya received an embassy from the Burmese king * who sought an alliance with the Siamese to subdue the Peguans (or

---

* King Mahadammayaza Dipati 1733-52

Mons) who had once again risen in revolt against the rule of Burma (1740). Although the Burman envoys were honorably received[66] no binding commitments seem to have been entered by the king of Siam. Indeed before long the two countries were once again engaged in mortal strife. In 1745-46 a return embassy sent by King Maha T'ammaraja II to the court of Ava* journeyed by hidden paths through teak forests because of the danger of attack by the Peguans. The Peguans in fact were in possession of large portions of the Irrawaddy Valley including the Minbu district. The Siamese envoys, therefore, advertised that they were the advance guard of a Thai army coming to the rescue of hard-pressed Ava. The ruse apparently succeeded. In the haughty atmosphere of the Ava court, however, the foreign envoys (notwithstanding the endeavors of the Burmese to effect an alliance with Siam) were kept waiting for a lengthy period— a gesture of Burman majesty designed to impress the Siamese envoys with their own insignificance. The Thai embassy after cooling its heels for a requisite period was finally granted an audience.[67] Nothing of note was accomplished on either side by the exchange of embassies.

King Maha T'ammaraja II, whatever his other faults, and they were numerously blatant, pursued a peaceful policy in intercourse with foreign nations redounding to the credit of the king and the repose of his kingdom. King Maha T'ammaraja II was also a great patron of the Buddhist religion, at least superficially, as seen in his relations with distant Ceylon. Kirti Soi (1747-81), the king of Kandy, also an avid patron of Buddhism, finding the hierarchy of the Buddhist church much decayed in his own country, dispatched an embassy to Siam in 1753 requesting monks be sent to Ceylon to help revitalize the Buddhist religion. A Ceylonese mission was also sent to Burma for similar purposes.[68] King Maha T'ammaraja II, flattered that such distant a potentate as the king of Kandy should deem the purity of faith in Siam worthy of emulation, dispatched a commission of fifteen Buddhist priests to Ceylon headed by a monk called Upali. The Thai mission returned to Siam claiming to have successfully purged Sinhalese Buddhism of its impurities. As a matter of fact the Upaliwong or Sayamwong sect claims the largest following among the Buddhist priests in Ceylon today; a sect which owes its origin to the religious zeal of the mission dispatched by King Maha T'ammaraja II.[69]

King Maha T'ammaraja II died in May 1758 at the age of seventy-seven.[70] His reign was peaceful, his subjects apparently content and the realm of Siam reasonably prosperous, suggesting the aptness of a panegyric echoing his state attainments. Actually the Kingdom of Ayudhya was entering the last period of a long decay, and the reign of King Maha T'ammaraja II was only a period of deceptive calm before the rages of a destructive storm. Certainly the reign of King Maha T'ammaraja II was not a period of progress as understood by the western application of the term. Indeed for Siam as for the rest of southeast Asia, the eighteenth century remained a period of stagnation at least in the techniques of physical production, and the improvements in the productive arts such as were revolutionizing life in Europe and America were noticeably absent in Siam. The people of Siam of the middle eighteenth century were caught between the clutches of an arbitrary king and a corrupt court. The population,

---

* Ava became the capital of Burma in 1634.

intent on the enjoyment of a prolonged peace, refused to prepare for the rigors and fatigues of war: a war once again to deluge Thailand in successive waves of Burman warriors, commencing with the renewal of the ancient struggle in 1760, and lasting well into the nineteenth century. The rise of the British East India Company as the paramount power in India culminating in the defeat of the Mahrattas in 1818, and a succession dispute in Assam, diverted Burmese attention to the west securing at least the western frontier of Siam from Burmese aggression, but also raising (for Siam) the spectre of a different imperialism when Burma was occupied by the British in three successive stages during the nineteenth century. We however defer such matters to their respective sequences, while resuming the narrative of eighteenth century Siam.

V. UT'UMP'ON (FIRST REIGN) 1758

Maha T'ammaraja II was survived by two sons of the first rank: Prince Ekat'at, the eldest son, and Prince Ut'ump'on, the youngest. The former, considered incapable by his father, also suffered from a disfiguring disease which may have been leprosy. The office of Maha Uparat was, therefore, bestowed by Maha T'ammaraja II on Prince Ut'ump'on.

King Ut'ump'on once in possession of the throne of Siam, signalized his brief three month reign by executing three half brothers, his immediate relations, who were collecting numerous armed retainers, and thus appeared to challenge the claim of King Ut'ump'on to the kingship. King Ut'ump'on, having secured one ingress to the precincts of his kingly office, found his brother, Prince Ekat'at, seeking to enter by a different entrance. Using a constant interference in the details of administration as a lever, Prince Ekat'at was able to pry loose the hinges of King Ut'ump'on's resistance. King Ut'ump'on, having cremated the body of his father, threw down his royal robes, donning the attire of a monk, and retired to the quietude of the Wat Pradu monastery, which he had recently constructed.[71] The incompetence of the new king, Ekat'at, who assumed the style of Boromoraja V, will be brought into clearer focus in the next chapter during our discussion of the Burmese wars, and the destruction of Ayudhya— kingdom, capital and city in the fatal year of 1767.

BIBLIOGRAPHY

1. Blankwaardt, W. "Notes upon the Relations between Holland and Siam," *Journal of the Siam Society*, Vol. VII, Bangkok, 1959.
2. Hall, D. G. E. *A History of South-East Asia*, MacMillan & Co., Ltd., London, and St. Martin's Press, New York, 1961.
3. Hamilton, Alexander. *A New Account of the East Indies*, Vol. II, The Argonaut Press, London, 1930.
4. Harvey, G. E. *History of Burma*, Longmans, Green and Co., London, 1925.
5. Hutchinson, E. W. "The Retirement of the French Garrison from Bangkok in the Year 1688," *Journal of the Siam Society*, Vol. VIII, Bangkok, 1959.
6. "Intercourse between Burma and Siam, as recorded in Hmannan Yazawindawgyi," *Journal of the Siam Society*, Vol. V, Part 1, Bangkok, 1959.
7. Kaempfer, Engelbert. *The History of Japan together with a Description of the Kingdom of Siam 1690-92*, Vol. I, James MacLehose and Sons, Glasgow, 1906. English translation by Scheuchzer, J. G.

8. Leclère, Adhémard. *Histoire du Cambodge*, Librairie Paul Geuthner, Paris, 1914.
9. Maybon, Charles B. *Histoire Moderne du Pays D'Annam (1592-1820)*, Typographie Plon-Nourrit et Cie, Paris, 1919.
10. *Records of the Relations between Siam and Foreign Countries in the 17th Century*, Printed by order of the Council of the Vajiranana National Library, Vol. V, Bangkok, 1921.
11. Russier, Henri. *Histoire Sommaire du Royaume de Cambodge*, Imprimerie Commerciale C. Ardin, Saigon, 1914.
12. Skinner, G. William. *Chinese Society in Thailand*, Cornell University Press, Ithaca, New York, 1957.
13. Turpin, François Henri. *History of the Kingdom of Siam*, Printed under the auspices of the Committee of the Vajiranana National Library, Bangkok, 1908. English translation by Cartwright, B. O.
14. Wood, W. A. R. *A History of Siam*, The Siam Barnakich Press, Bangkok, 1933.

FOOTNOTES

1. Hutchinson, 164.
2. Ibid., 193.
3. Ibid., 164.
4. Ibid., 194.
5. Ibid.
6. Ibid., 164.
7. Ibid.
8. Hutchinson, 166, and Hall, 312.
9. Hutchinson, 193, 194.
10. Turpin, 99.
11. Ibid., 99-103.
12. Records, etc., 66-68.
13. Hutchinson, 168.
14. Wood, 218.
15. Hall, 312-14.
16. Wood, 214.
17. Ibid., 216.
18. Kaempfer, 37.
19. Turpin, 111.
20. Hall, 386.
21. Wood, 220.
22. Ibid., 220, 221.
23. Ibid., 221.
24. Ibid. The various authorities of southeast Asian history do not concur in the reignal years of the king of Cambodia in 1697. Wood states King Sadet Jai Jett'a reigned in Cambodia, 1690-1716 with intervals, and that he was the king of Cambodia who made the presentation of the white elephant; See Wood, 221. But Russier places Chey Chettah IV, presumably the same monarch as Wood's Sadet Jai Jett'a, on the Cambodian throne, 1675-1706 with intervals; See Russier's King Lists III. In the King Lists of Hall, Chettha IV ruled Cambodia 1675-1702; See Hall, 740.

25. Hall, 314.
26. Wood, 221, 222.
27. Ibid., 222.
28. Records, etc., 159.
29. Wood, 223. Turpin declares King P'etraja was succeeded by his son in 1700; See Turpin, 111.
30. Wood, 224. According to Turpin: "Pitracha [P'etraja], seated on a throne defiled with the blood of the royal family combined in himself all the talents of great men with all the vices of the vilest scoundrels."; See Turpin, 109.
31. Wood, 223, 224. The younger half brother of King P'rachao Sua, Tras Noi, ordained as a priest, apparently died a natural death; See Wood, 223.
32. Turpin, 111.
33. Wood, 225, 226.
34. Ibid., 225.
35. Turpin, 111, 112.
36. Ibid., 112.
37. Blankwaardt, 27, 28.
38. Wood, 226.
39. Ibid., 227.
40. Hall, 387, and Russier, 91, 92. Wood states that the first ten years of T'ai Sra's (Pu'mint'araja's) reign were peaceful, and that he did not intervene in Cambodian affairs until 1717; See Wood, 227. I notice Leclère states the reignal years of King Thommo-Reachea (apparently Prea Srey Thomea) as 1702-04 and 1706-10, and the reignal years of Kevhvea Angk Em (apparently Keo Fa) as 1700-01 and 1710-22; See Leclère, 366-70. In the King Lists of Russier Thommo Racha reigned in 1702 and again in 1706-10. The reignal years of Ang-Em, Leclère's Kevhvea Angk Em, are given as 1699-1701 and 1710-22; See Russier's King Lists III. Russier states that Ang-Em (Keo Fa) profited by a revolt of immigrant Laotians to call in a Vietnamese army to help him expel King Thommo Racha (Prea Srey Thomea) in 1710; See Russier, 91, 92. However Maybon places the expulsion of King Prea Srey Thomea from his throne by Em (Keo Fa) in 1714; See Maybon, 123-25. Relying on Maybon and also Hall I have placed the overthrow of Prea Srey Thomea in the year 1714.
41. Wood, 227.
42. Hamilton, 97.
43. Ibid., 105, 106. Maybon states the Siamese fleet was destroyed by a storm. Maybon's account of the southern expedition in general agrees with the account by Captain Hamilton although, as I have stated in the text, Hamilton was not aware of the progress of the northern army under P'ya Chakri; See Maybon, 123-25.
44. Wood, 227, 228.
45. Ibid., 228.
46. Wood, 229, 230, and "Intercourse, etc.," 184.
47. Wood, 228, 229. Turpin states he died of cancer of the throat; See Turpin, 115, 116.
48. Wood, 229.

49. Turpin, 116, and Wood, 231.
50. Turpin, 116.
51. Wood, 231.
52. Turpin, 117.
53. Ibid., 117, 118.
54. Wood, 231.
55. Turpin, 118, 119.
56. Ibid., 121, 122.
57. Ibid., 119, 120.
58. Ibid., 120.
59. Ibid., 120, 121.
60. Wood, 232.
61. Skinner, 19.
62. Ibid., 8, 9.
63. Ibid., 11.
64. Turpin, 122, 123.
65. Wood, 237. Turpin states the Maha Uparat was imprisoned for life; See Turpin, 123.
66. Wood, 234, 235.
67. Harvey, 214.
68. Hall, 388.
69. Wood, 237.
70. Ibid., 238.
71. Ibid., 237-39.

CHAPTER FIVE

THE LATE AYUDHYA PERIOD 1629 - 1767 — PART 3
UNTIL THE BURMESE DESTRUCTION OF AYUDHYA IN 1767

I. BOROMORAJA V OR EKAT'AT (FIRST REIGN) 1758-60

While the Kingdom of Siam bathed in the repose of a prolonged tranquility, Burma, the ancient enemy, writhed in the turmoil of her own disunity—the offspring of the pusillanimity of the last kings of the Toungoo dynasty. We merely add (in brief description) that kings of the calibre of Minrekyawdin (1673-98), Sane (1698-1714), Taninganwe (1714-33) and Mahadammayaza Dipati (1733-52) ruled Burma with consummate weakness while the fortunes of the Burmese state reached a recurring low ebb reflecting the dynastic debility of the Burman monarchy—the one-time imperial instrument of Tabinshwehti (1531-50) and Bayinnaung (1551-81). Indeed during the reign of King Mahadammayaza Dipati the stricken Burmese kingdom labored successively under the blows of a foreign intruder and the scourge of the oft-repeated Mon revolt.

Throughout the first half of the eighteenth century the agile horsemen of the mountain state of Manipur raided west Burma, reaching the banks of the Irrawaddy at Sagaing in 1738. Plunder, not conquest, lured the men of Manipur, and neither the king of Burma, nor his liegemen, could prevent periodic sweeps of the Manipuri horsemen and the destruction of Burmese villages and pagodas.

The impotence of the Burmese monarchy confronted by the foreign intruder encouraged the perennially dissatisfied Mon population to rise in rebellion. The cities of Syriam, Martaban and Pegu were seized by the Mons who invested Smim Htaw Buddhaketi (1740-47) with the kingship of a resurrected Kingdom of Pegu. Burmese attempts to subdue the rebels proved ineffectual, and the Mons commenced raiding northward along the Irrawaddy. However, King Smim Htaw Buddhaketi, although popular with his subjects, was nevertheless an incompetent ruler. In 1747, following a Mon defeat, the king of Pegu quitted his uncongenial royal station retiring to Chiengmai with a strong guard. Binnya Dala (1747-57), the chief minister of Smim Htaw Buddhaketi, was elected to the vacated throne and envisioned not the mere indepedence of his own Pegu, but an empire of greater dimensions. In 1751 a large Mon army, equipped with European arms, commanded by General Talaban—of considerable repute among the Mon population—invaded Upper Burma capturing Ava in April 1752 and deposing King Mahadammayaza Dipati, the last king of the Toungoo dynasty.[1]

At the modern town of Shwebo, northwest of Mandalay, the Burmese leader, Alaungpaya (1752-60), rallied the dispirited Burmese, reforging their warlike ardor, and rooting the Konbaung dynasty, which ruled Burma until 1885, in the soil of Upper Burma. In 1755 King Alaungpaya defeated the Mons in a decisive engagement at Lunhse. He renamed the town Myanaung or "Speedy Victory." In the same year King Alaungpaya commenced work on the foundations of a new city, Rangoon or "The End of Strife" in anticipation of the reunion of the severed portions of the kingdom of his predecessors. However, Pegu, and its port Syriam, the entrepot of European trade, remained unsubdued.[2] But not for long. Having secured his interests in the north, King Alaungpaya commenced the siege of Pegu, capturing the capital city in May 1757.[3] Binnya Dala, the king of Pegu, was captured, but escaped with his life, although not his person.[*][4] The reincarnation of the old Kingdom of Pegu expired after an eventful, albeit brief, seventeen years of existence. King Alaungpaya having established his supremacy in Burma, and created an army inured to martial enterprise, could now assay the role of conqueror in Thailand. A pretext for war against the Kingdom of Siam was not wanting in the activities of Mon refugees in Siam who made incursions into Burmese territory on the Tavoy frontier.[5] (The Burmese captured Tavoy from the Mon rebels in 1759.) [6] Phayre states King Alaungpaya was also incensed against the Siamese king because the latter would not grant in marriage one of his daughters to the sovereign lord of Burma.[7]

With or without credible pretexts for launching aggressive war against the kingdom of Boromoraja V, King Alaungpaya fancied his own regal endowments justified a predilection to recreate the once far-flung imperial edifice of King Bayinnaung to which had been appended the Kingdom of Ayudhya (1569-84), in meek subservience, at the foot of the Burman throne. Having, therefore, determined upon war with his eastern neighbor, King Alaungpaya assembled a large army at Rangoon for his Siamese expedition. King Alaungpaya, and his son the prince of Myedu, the future Hsinbyushin (1763-76), departed Rangoon with an army of forty regiments, presumably of all arms,[**] for Hanthawadi (Pegu) in January 1760. A small Burmese army, including a regiment of Kala Panthes (Portuguese), was dispatched to Dawe (Tavoy) in five ships. The combined forces may have contained sixty thousand men.

The main Burman army, arriving at Hanthawadi (Pegu), marched to Mottama (Martaban) where a portion of the army embarked by boat for Dawe (Tavoy). The remainder of the forces crossed the Salween River to Mawlanyaing (Moulmein) by raft and boat, in the company of King Alaungpaya, and then marched to Dawe (Tavoy). After gathering in the seaborne detachments, transported from Rangoon and Mottama (Martaban), the entire Burmese army marched to Byeik (Mergui) in Siamese territory. The Burman advance guard consisted of three hundred horse and three thousand men under Mingaung Nawrata, and five hundred horse and five thousand men led by the prince of Myedu. Byeik (Mergui) and two days later the port city of Taninthari (Tenasserim) were occupied with little or no resistance.[8]

The Siamese little expected a Burmese attack from the south. Three Thai armies had moved to guard the western passes, but they were outflanked from the south. An army of twenty thousand men, however, watched for Burmese activity in the Peninsula.[9]

The Burman army after a five day march from Taninthari (Tenasserim) skirmished with Ayudhyan advance forces near the town of Kwi (Kui Nua). The Siamese were forced to retire, Mingaung Nawrata following close on Thai heels.[10] The Burmese had apparently traversed the Peninsula by way of the Maw Daung Pass. After debouching on the Gulf of Siam, King Alaungpaya marched northward.[11] Byat-pi (P'etchaburi) and Ratbi (Ratburi) were captured by the Burmese army. Again little or no resistance was offered to the invaders. From Ratbi (Ratburi) the triumphal Burman procession marched

---

* Binnya Dala was executed by King Hsinbyushin (1763-76) in 1774.
** Men, horse and elephants

toward the sea, via Ban-Lwin (Bang Rachan?). A Siamese force comprising fifteen regiments with two hundred elephants, one thousand horse and twenty thousand men commanded by Aukbya Yazawunthan (presumably the P'ya Yomarat of Wood) intercepted the Burmese line of march. The Ayudhyans were overthrown when the forces of the prince of Myedu (in support of Mingaung Nawrata and Minhla Nawrata, who were being worsted by the Siamese), turned the tide of battle in favor of the Burmese. The routed Ayudhyans lost one hundred elephants and two thousand men.[12]

II. UT'UMP'ON (SECOND REIGN) 1760-62

Wood states consternation reigned at Ayudhya when the defeats of the Siamese armies registered in the public consciousness. King Boromoraja V was blamed for the poor showing of the Siamese forces, and Ut'ump'on was recalled to the throne * amid prospects of incipient disaster.[13]

About the time Ut'ump'on resumed the reins of government, King Alaungpaya forced the Talan River (near Sup'an). The prince of Myedu personally conducted the fording of the river in three columns of Burman troops.** A Siamese force opened a heavy fire, repulsing the Burman assailants until King Alaungpaya, marching to the river with royal standards unfurled—amidst the martial beat of drums and gongs, intervened at the decisive moment precipitating the overthrow of the Ayudhyan army commanded by Aukbya Kalahon (P'ya Kalahom). The *Hmannan Yazawin Dawgyi* estimates the Thai army consisted of three hundred elephants, three thousand horse and thirty thousand men divided into six brigades. Resting for three days at a nearby village, the Burmese marched on Ayudhya arriving at the capital in April 1760. King Alaungpaya encamped to the north of the city.[14]

Although King Alaungpaya had trampled all Thai opposition before him, he now butted his head against the walls of Ayudhya in vain. King Ut'ump'on resolved to withstand the Burmese onslaught as best he could, confiding in the rains to inundate the Burmese camp and force their withdrawal. While making preparations for a vigorous resistance, if necessary, King Ut'ump'on was not unwilling to effect a compromise solution, dispatching messengers to apprise His Burman Majesty of his willingness to recognize the suzerainty of Burma. King Alaungpaya had the temerity to state his purpose in marching to Ayudhya was engendered by a tender solicitude for the advancement of Buddhism. The king of Burma requested a meeting with the Ayudhyan king. No meeting occurred— King Ut'ump'on undoubtedly meriting the proposal with the contempt it deserved.[15]

The advent of the rainy season was a prime factor which weakened the Burmese resolution to persist in the siege of Ayudhya. Both Thai and Burmese accounts, however, differ as to the immediate cause of the Burmese withdrawal. Wood states King Alaungpaya received severe injuries when a cannon burst (the king himself was superintending the loading of a cannon aimed at the Royal Palace).[16] The *Hmannan Yazawin Dawgyi*, however, asserts King Alaungpaya suddenly felt indisposed—scarcely a graphic account of his ailment. A council

---

* Prince Damrong states Boromoraja V invited Ut'ump'on to ascend the throne.
** Minhla Nawrata commanded the left column, Minhla Thiri the center and Mingaung Nawrata the right column.

of the king's liegemen was convened at which his son, the prince of Myedu, doubted the sincerity of the Siamese offer of submission, declaring the offer a mere ruse to gain time until the rains inundated the countryside. King Alaungpaya, moved by anxiety for his health and in deference to the wishes of his commanders, decided to withdraw from the Kingdom of Siam. The siege was raised in May of 1760, and the army of King Alaungpaya marched toward Burma—Mingaung Nawrata forming the rear guard.[17]

Both Phayre and Wood indicate King Alaungpaya (carried in a litter) retired by the northern route via Rahaeng and Myawadi.[18] King Alaungpaya, however, died in May 1760 before reaching the Salween River. The great Burman warrior was forty years of age at the time of his death,[19] renowned both for his conquests and the establishment of the Konbaung dynasty which ruled Burma until the British conquest in 1885.

"The danger through which they had passed failed to teach the Siamese the necessity for union. King Ut'ump'on, who had thought that his resumption of the crown was to be permanent, soon found his brother [Boromoraja V] intriguing against him, and in 1762, fearing that his life was in danger, he retired once more to his monastery.

"The indifference of the Siamese to the Burmese peril was fostered by the difficulties in which Manglok [Naungdawgyi, 1760-63], the eldest son and successor of Alaungpaya, found himself. Rebels rose up against him on every side, and for two years he was forced to fight for his throne. By the year 1762 he had, however, gained control over his whole realm, with the exception of Tavoy, which was under the rule of one Huit'ongcha [Shwe Taungza in Burmese history]."[20]

III. BOROMORAJA V OR EKAT'AT (SECOND REIGN) 1762-67

King Naungdawgyi of Burma dispatched his lieutenant, Abaya Kamani, with a force of eight thousand men to re-add Zinme (Chiengmai), the sometime Burmese vassal, to the patrimony of his predecessors. The expedition realized its purpose.[21] Chiengmai was occupied in July 1763, before a Siamese army commanded by P'ya P'itsanulok, could effectually answer an appeal for aid.[22]

In December 1763 after the death of Naungdawgyi, the prince of Myedu, the second son of Alaungpaya, ascended the throne of Burma. The conqueror of Ayudhya and oppressor of the Thais is known to history as King Hsinbyushin (1763-76) or Lord of the White Elephant.[23] His aggressive policy precipitated Burmese wars with Manipur, Luang Prabang * and even China as well as the Kingdom of Siam. But first King Hsinbyushin had to quell a revolt in Chiengmai. In March 1764 the king of Burma dispatched Nemyo Thihapate with a force of twenty thousand men to subdue the recalcitrant principality. Having accomplished the lesser charge Nemyo Thihapate was ordered to proceed to Linzin (Luang Prabang) and effect the conquest of that state in preparation to march against the Kingdom of Ayudhya.[24]

---

* In 1707 the Kingdom of Lang Chang (Laos), founded by Fa Ngum in 1353, was divided into two separate kingdoms, Vien Chang (Vientiane) and Luang Prabang, as the result of succession disputes.

"As soon as he [King Hsinbyushin] had made the arrangements described above, he said to his ministers that Yodaya
[Ayudhya] had never before been utterly destroyed and crip-
pled, and therefore it might not be possible to attain the
object in view with only such forces as were under Nemyo
Thihapate sent via Zinme [Chiengmai]. He said that, to
expedite the success of the expedition, a force was necessary
to enter Yodaya [Ayudhya] by way of Dawe [Tavoy] and
accordingly ordered that a force composed of 20 regiments
of infantry containing 100 elephants and 20,000 men, and
10 squadrons of cavalry containing 1,000 horse, be sent via
Dawe [Tavoy] under the supreme command of Maha Nawrata with Nemyo Gonnarat and Tuyin Yan-aung-gyaw as sec-
onds in command. This force left the capital [Shwebo] on the
8th of [the] waxing Nadaw 1126 (December A.D. 1764)." [25]

Early in 1765 King Hsinbyushin successfully raided the mountain state of
Manipur (west of Burma) with an army of forty thousand men enslaving nearly
the entire population of the capital city while his generals, Nemyo Thihapate
and Maha Nawrata, were carving spheres of Burmese influence on the eastern
frontiers.

Nemyo Thihapate re-established the Burmese supremacy in Zinme (Chiengmai) without much ado, quartering his troops at Anan (Nan) for the duration
of the rainy season (1764). In November 1764 Nemyo Thihapate commenced
operations against the Kingdom of Luang Prabang. The Burmese defeated the
Luang Prabang forces on the west bank of the Me Kaung (Mekong) opposite
Maing-Lon (Luang Prabang). Maing-Lon (Luang Prabang) was taken by assault ca. January 1765, and the king of Luang Prabang was laid under a heavy
contribution being forced to recognize the suzerainty of King Hsinbyushin as
well. The Burmese army departed Maing-Lon (Luang Prabang) in April 1765
arriving at Lagun (Lamp'ang) in May where the Burmese established headquarters for the rainy season (1765).[26] King Hsinbyushin could view with
satisfaction the performance of his warriors, but the foremost embellishment of
the Burmese military art we have yet to record.

Two Burmese armies were poised on the frontiers of Siam prepared to
deliver the *coup de grâce* to the old Kingdom of Ayudhya. We must now relate
the circumstances of that downfall terminating in the cruel sack and overthrow
of the old city of Ayudhya—consumed in a conflagration whose hot blast temporarily rent Siam asunder. The various written records of the old kingdom were
all but destroyed, and the very memory of Ayudhya was threatened with extinction, a fate happily averted—but to continue our narrative.

The Burmese South Army after making full preparations for the enterprise
of Ayudhya set forth from Tavoy late in the year 1765.

"When the rains were over the Burmese army was augmented
by the addition of the following forces which came to Dawe
[Tavoy], namely, 3,000 men formed into six regiments under
the command of Einda Yaza (Indaraja) from Hanthawadi
[Pegu], 3,000 men also in six regiments under the command
of Binnya Sein from Mottama [Martaban], and four regi-

ments of 2,000 men from Taninthari [Tenasserim] and Byeik [Mergui*] under the command of Lakyawdin, while four regiments of 2,000 men levied in Dawe [Tavoy] were placed under the command of the Governor of Mottama [Martaban]. The total of the forces after the addition of the levies amounted to 200 elephants, 2,000 horse, and 30,000 men. This army left Dawe [Tavoy] for Yodaya [Ayudhya] on the 10th of [the] waxing Tazaungmon 1127 (November A.D. 1765)."[27]

The Burmese army apparently marched by the same route followed by Alaungpaya in 1760 (we assumed Alaungpaya crossed the Peninsula by the Maw Daung Pass).** The Burmese captured Byat-pi (P'etchaburi) by storm, looted the city and leaving a small garrison in occupation, marched to Ratbi (Ratburi) which fell to the Burmese without resistance—the governor meekly tendering submission to the conquering Burmese as did the principal officials. General Maha Nawrata thereupon issued orders that the inhabitants of the city should not be molested in their persons or property. When the Burmese army approached Kanpuri (Kanburi) the governor, who was well supplied with food and arms, decided not to submit. But to no avail. The city was captured by assault with the usual scenes of looting. Other cities were captured offering little or no resistance.[28]

King Boromoraja V, apprised of the approach of the Burmese, dispatched an army which, according to the *Hmannan Yazawin Dawgyi*, numbered five hundred elephants, and an equal number of cannon mounted on carriages and sixty thousand men. The Ayudhyan army prepared to make a stand at a place called Thigok by the Burmese (not far from Sup'an), west of Ayudhya. The Burmese cavalry descried the Thai army. The Burmese army attacked the Siamese frontally disregarding tactical niceties. A sanguinary struggle ensued in which the Burmese bludgeoned holes in the Ayudhyan defensive line forcing a disastrous retreat.[29]

> "Over a hundred elephants and 200 cannons were captured, and over 2,000 men made prisoners. The Burmese did not follow up the retreating army, but turned their attention to the town of Thigok, which they stormed and captured together with its governor. The oath of allegiance was given to the principal officials while the governor was held a pris-

---

* Mergui and Tenasserim were, until the renewal of the Burmese wars, Siamese territory. Prince Damrong states the Burmese captured, prior to the march to Ayudhya, the towns of Maliwun, Ranong, Chumphon and Chaiya.

** The route of the Maw Daung Pass (south), the Three Pagodas Pass (center) and the Me Sot route (north) are the three natural points of entry on the Burmese frontier for the invasion of the Ayudhyan Kingdom. Since the Burmese assembled their forces at Dawe (Tavoy) in 1765, far south of the Three Pagodas Pass, we reasonably assume they did not mean to retrace their steps and march northward to enter Siam by the Three Pagodas Pass, but meant to press southward, enter the Maw Daung Pass, and approach Yodaya (Ayudhya) from the south.

oner. Then leaving a small force to hold the town, the Burmese marched towards Yodaya [Ayudhya], and encamped at Kanni village, to the west of the capital and within five days' march from it. A message was sent to His Burman Majesty conveying the news that all the towns to the west of Yodaya [Ayudhya] had been captured and that the Burmese army was encamped at Kanni village. They decided to give full rest to the forces and wait for the arrival of the army which was coming through Zinme [Chiengmai]." [30]

Prince Damrong states Maha Nawrata while at Ratburi organized a sea force under a certain Mekhara Bo who attacked the cities of T'onburi and Nont'aburi east of the line of march of the Burmese South Army. Powney, the captain of an English merchant ship, volunteered to assist the Siamese in the defense of T'onburi, but to no avail. Captain Powney retreated with his vessel to Ayudhya. Arriving at Ayudhya, Captain Powney requested and received larger guns to attack the Burmese near Nont'aburi. The Englishman bombarded the Burmese position below Nont'aburi doing great execution, but the Burmese were not to be denied and the British vessel was obliged to proceed down river to the open sea. P'ya Yomaraj (Yomarat), the Siamese general defending Nont'aburi, withdrew to Ayudhya. The Burman naval force met with no resistance on proceeding to the doomed city arriving at the capital in January 1766 about the same time as Maha Nawrata established his camp to the west of the capital. [31]

While the communications of Ayudhya were being severed in the west and south, the army of Nemyo Thihapate was moving to invest Ayudhya from the north. The North Army marched from Lagun (Lamp'ang) for Yodaya (Ayudhya) in November 1765, augmented by contingents from Zinme (Chiengmai) and Linzin (Luang Prabang). According to the *Hmannan Yazawin Dawgyi* the Burmese army contained fifty-eight regiments consisting of three hundred war boats, four hundred elephants, twelve hundred horse and forty-three thousand men.

The Burmese occupied a place called Ban Tet (Burmese designation) and received the submission of Kamanpaik (Kamphaeng Phet) before assaulting Thuwunkalauk (Sawankaloke) which was rapidly engulfed in the Burmese tide of conquest. Thaukkate (Sukhothai) and Peikthalauk (P'itsanulok) were plucked from the feeble hand of Boromoraja V with scant resistance. When the Burmese arrived at Peikthalauk (P'itsanulok) ten regiments commanded by Thiri Nanda Thingyan and another ten regiments led by Kyawgaung Kyawthu scoured the Thai countryside. Many Siamese towns submitted to the Burmese without the rudeness of resistance—bespeaking the pusillanimity of the latter-day Ayudhyans. The Burmese proceeded to commandeer horses, elephants and men from the towns and cities occupied along the line of march, forming a new division of thirteen regiments. The hapless Siamese were forced to march in the van of the Burmese army now seventy-one regiments strong. The *Hmannan Yazawin Dawgyi*, unfortunately, does not state the Burmese line of march. About three miles northeast of Ayudhya, however, a battle was fought in which the redoubtable Burmans once again overthrew a large Siamese force near a place called Pananpathok (Burmese designation). [32] The final siege of Ayudhya commenced in February 1766, and terminated fourteen months later amid scenes of irrevocable ruin and devastation; the handiwork of a merciless foe whose malignity refused to spare objects devoted to the sanctity of a common faith. Old Ayudhya was never rebuilt.

The Siamese, whose progenitors had overthrown many Burman armies in times past, were but poorly provided in the art of self-defense, in harsh terms related by Turpin as follows:

> "While the Burmese, scattered over all the provinces, were carrying on a war against men and nature, the King and his superstitious ministers put all their trust in their magicians. The officers and soldiers followed their example and consulted them as to how they might render themselves invisible in order to attack the enemy unawares, and the hope of learning a secret so favourable to their cowardly nature, prevented them from going out to fight before it had been revealed to them. . . .
>
> The leaders, on a par with the subordinates as regards valour, appeared to have taken up arms against their fellow citizens only. They robbed them of their money and food with the excuse that they were required for the use of the military to whom they distributed the least valuable part of their spoil, but this bounty was merely to cloak their own extortions. Whilst the more wealthy citizens were being ruined, the vigilance of the missionaries foresaw the destitution of the Christians, but their liberality, extended without exception to all creeds, [and] exhausted their supplies. The Burmese intercepted all their [the Siamese] convoys and they themselves were in danger of famine owing to the excess of their ravages. The forces sent against them were invariably dispersed and frequently returned without striking a blow." [33]

King Boromoraja V first ordered sorties against Nemyo Thihapate encamped near the eastern walls of the city, and then against Maha Nawrata west of Ayudhya. Both attacks were repulsed.[34] But:

> "The city of Yodaya [Ayudhya] was so surrounded by rivers and other water-ways that the Burmese found it difficult to approach the city walls. They decided to [completely] invest it by pitching camps round it. The forces of the column which had come from the south via Dawe [Tavoy] were distributed as follows: Nemyo Gonnarat, Mingyi Zeyathu and Kamani Sanda each with seven regiments were stationed on the western face of the city; Kemayaza, Yanngu Thiri Kyawdin and Minnge Bala each with seven regiments were on the southern face. The northern column which had come by way of Zinme [Chiengmai] was disposed of as follows: twenty-five regiments under four commanders on the eastern face of the city, and twenty-one regiments under three commanders on the northern face. There were 88 regiments on

the four sides of the city. Several attempts were made to assail the city by approaching the walls, but without success, and the reasons given for the failure were that the moat round the city was very deep and wide; that the walls were very high and very strongly built; that a river had to be crossed before any attack could be made; that the guns mounted on the ramparts were numerous and the fire so effective that they could not get even near the walls." [35]

While the Burmese besieged the capital the Siamese, inefficient as they were, were not altogether inactive in the outlying districts of the kingdom. Prince Damrong states the Burmese were much harassed by a Thai guerrilla army at Bang Rachan. In July 1766, after five months vigorous resistance, the brave villagers of Bang Rachan were attacked and overwhelmed by the Burmese who had failed to subdue the stalwart villagers in seven previous attempts. [36]

As the rainy season approached certain of the Burmese commanders suggested raising the siege of Ayudhya. But such views were anathema to the warlike Maha Nawrata appointed commander-in-chief about this time. To raise the siege of Ayudhya, Maha Nawrata suggested, would be like liberating fish enmeshed in a net. [37]

"His plan was to seize all the provisions obtainable in the neighbourhood, to cultivate rice with the buffaloes and bullocks seized, to send their horses and elephants to some high grazing ground, and to build forts in places where the water was low and to station outposts between the forts as a means of communication between them. This plan was approved. ... About five days after they had started work the water rose very high." [38]

The Siamese continued their sorties against the Burmese, but with as little success as before. [39] In September the Burmese seized a strong position which enabled their artillery to command a section of the river near Ayudhya. The Dutch quarter was threatened with capture. Turpin states the Christians of Ayudhya made valiant efforts to defend their various compounds, but by December 1766 their situation was desperate. In that month, or shortly after, the Dutch quarter fell to the Burmese after an eight day siege and was reduced to ashes.* The Portuguese among the Christians of Ayudhya seem to have displayed the foremost valor. [40] Turpin, as we have seen, breathes contempt for the Siamese efforts at defense, but the *Hmannan Yazawin Dawgyi*, in fairer judgment, states many Thai sorties, although unsuccessful, were nevertheless conducted with vigor and resource. The Siamese artillery, as the Burmese chronicler has told us, was well served. The very length of the siege (14 months) indicates the population of the doomed city did prepare and execute a determined resistance. The hardships which the common people endured is proof again the Siamese, whatever their military incapacity, were determined to resist

---

* The Dutch settlement at Ayudhya was situated on the south side of the capital. The destruction of the Dutch factory in 1767 terminated the connection of the Dutch East India Company with Siam. Dutch relations with Siam remained in abeyance for nearly a century.

the Burmese aggression to the bitter end, notwithstanding a corrupt and venial officialdom. Food was virtually unobtainable. The poor awaited death to terminate their misery. An epidemic scourged the city while corpses rotted in the streets.[41] Yet the tortured city still bid defiance to the Burmese whose advance had overrun the outlying portions of Ayudhya enabling the Burmese to range their artillery against the interior of the city.* [42]

Amid the belching of flame and smoke we can well imagine the Burmese were not too particular how they directed the fire of their batteries. Although King Boromoraja V sought to avert the fated doom by propitiating an offer of vassalage to His Burman Majesty, Hsinbyushin, such sounds were the mere rumblings of the death rattle of expiring Ayudhya. Nor did the death of the Burmese commander-in-chief, Maha Nawrata, avert the inevitable fate which now awaited the old kingdom. King Hsinbyushin merely gnashed and gnawed, ordering an all out effort to dispatch the stricken prey caught within his grasp. When captured, King Hsinbyushin ordered the Burmese commanders to raze Ayudhya to the ground. To help expedite matters King Hsinbyushin deputed Minye Minhla Uzana, the governor of Mottama (Martaban), with an additional three thousand men to replace Maha Nawrata in command of the Dawe (Tavoy) column.** The reinforcements were commanded to march as rapidly as possible to the Siamese capital. The small force left Ava in February 1767.*** [43]

The Burmese made their final assault on Ayudhya in April of 1767. The defenses on the northern side of Ayudhya had been weakened by tunnels evacuated under the walls of the city.

"Then with firewood and other inflammable materials, the wooden posts and beams supporting the base of the walls in the tunnels were set fire to. Owing to the heat cracks were formed in the overlying ground; and the posts supporting the wall having been burnt away, about a hundred "tas" [****] of the wall collapsed. The Burmese forces then made a general rush, some entered the city through the breach thus caused, some scaled the walls with ladders and got inside, while others also made their entry by three tunnels leading into the city. The Siamese nobles tried their best to exhort the defenders to fight with all their might, but owing to their having been on reduced rations for a considerable time, the resistance was feeble and ineffectual. As soon as the Burmese gained a footing in the city they set fire to the houses, public buildings, monasteries, and other religious edifices. The Burmese soldiery seized men, women, gold, silver, jewels, etc., and

---

* To add to the misery of the inhabitants a great fire in Ayudhya consumed ten thousand houses in January 1767.

** We may assume Nemyo Thihapate received the supreme command, although confirmation is lacking in the version of the *Hmannan Yazawin Dawgyi* I have used in this work.

*** Ayudhya was captured before the force of Minye Min-hla Uzana could reach the capital.

**** One Ta equals seven cubits; one cubit equals about twenty inches.

confusion and disorder reigned supreme." [44]

King Boromoraja V fled from the scene of utter ruin which encompassed his capital. Wood speculates he died from hunger and exposure after wandering in the jungle.[45] The *Hmannan Yazawin Dawgyi* declares Ekadat (King Boromoraja V) was killed by a random shot amid the wild confusion of a ruthless sack and the destruction of Ayudhya.[46] The ex-king, Ut'ump'on, was pulled from his temple, and taken to Burma where he died a captive in 1796.[47] The victors procured a prodigious loot of slaves and booty of all kinds.

> "All the largest and most beautiful images of Buddha were hacked in pieces, and many of them were burnt for the sake of the gold leaf with which they were coated. Plunder, and still more plunder, was the watchword. Men, women and children were flogged and tortured to make them reveal the hiding-places where their few treasures or savings were concealed." * [48]

Having satiated a ferocious appetite, or perhaps devoured in the manner of locusts all that the land grew, the main army of the conquerors left Ayudhya in June 1767 westward plodding its weary way.[49] Only the charred ruins, testimony to the savagery of the victors, remained of the ancient capital the proud city of Ayudhya, as palls of smoke billowed their own tale of woe and the jungle rains helped to quench the enmity of bitter memories. A hush descended over the old city whose roads and canals had echoed many a triumph; many a knightly act as well as deed of treachery. Silence disturbed by the sounds of the jungle settled upon the ruins, quickly engulfed by a sea of vegetation. The New Ayudhya which arose is but a pale reflection of the glory of the old city whose story we have related.

---

* In addition to the human misery and material destruction the historian must lament the destruction of the Siamese records which were consumed by the fires which tortured the old city in the agony of death. For many years it seemed as though all indigenous record of ancient Siam had vanished with that pulse of Ayudhya which in ages past beat so rapidly. Piece by piece, however, the fragments of the story of the old kingdom were found, and transcribed in the *P'ongsawadan* chronicles, albeit with many errors, but also with many essential truths. The discovery of the *Luang Prasoet* chronicle in 1907 has provided the historian with a yet surer foundation for elucidating Siamese history.

BIBLIOGRAPHY

1. Damrong, Prince. "Our Wars with the Burmese," *Journal of the Burma Research Society,* Vol. XL, Part II (a), Rangoon, 1958.
2. Hall, D. G. E. *A History of South-East Asia,* MacMillan & Co., Ltd., London, and St. Martin's Press, New York, 1961.
3. "Intercourse between Burma and Siam, as Recorded in Hmannan Yazawindawgyi," *Journal of the Siam Society,* Vol. VI, Part 2, Bangkok, 1959.
4. Phayre, Sir Arthur P. *History of Burma,* Trubner & Co., London, 1883.
5. Turpin, François Henri. *History of the Kingdom of Siam,* Printed under the auspices of the Committee of the Vajiranana National Library, Bangkok, 1908. English translation by Cartwright, B. O.

6. Wood, W. A. R. *A History of Siam*, The Siam Barnakich Press, Bangkok, 1933.

FOOTNOTES

1. Hall, 324-27.
2. Ibid., 343, 344.
3. Ibid., 347, 348.
4. Wood, 236, 237.
5. Phayre, 168.
6. Wood, 240.
7. Phayre, 168.
8. "Intercourse, etc.," 4-6.
9. Wood, 240, 241.
10. "Intercourse, etc.," 6.
11. Phayre, 169.
12. "Intercourse, etc.," 6, 7.
13. Wood, 241.
14. "Intercourse, etc.," 7-9.
15. Ibid., 10.
16. Wood, 241, 242.
17. "Intercourse, etc.," 11, 12.
18. Phayre, 170, and Wood, 242.
19. Phayre, 170. The Burmese were harassed by the Siamese during the retreat, but the endeavors of the Ayudhyan army to trap Mingaung Nawrata (with the Burmese rear guard) at a place the Burmese call Ban Tun, were unsuccessful, notwithstanding the greater size of the Siamese army which the *Hmannan Yazawin Dawgyi* tells us suffered a complete defeat; See "Intercourse, etc.," 12, 13. Wood states the Siamese harassed their adversaries all the way to Burma; See Wood, 242.
20. Wood, 242.
21. "Intercourse, etc.," 17, 18.
22. Wood, 243.
23. "Intercourse, etc.," 17, 18.
24. Ibid., 18, 19.
25. Ibid., 19, 20. Tavoy was occupied without difficulty. The rebel governor fled, receiving the protection of Siam; See Wood, 243.
26. "Intercourse, etc.," 20-23.
27. Ibid., 23.
28. Ibid., 24, 25. Wood states the Burmese, previous to the successful invasion from the south, attempted to occupy P'etchaburi but were repulsed by P'ya Tak—the future King Taksin (1767-82)—and obliged to withdraw, retreating to Tenasserim; See Wood, 243, 244.
29. "Intercourse, etc.," 26.
30. Ibid.
31. Prince Damrong, 320-22.
32. "Intercourse, etc.," 26-29.
33. Turpin, 161.
34. "Intercourse, etc.," 30-32.

35. Ibid., 33, 34.
36. Prince Damrong, 327-29.
37. "Intercourse, etc.," 34.
38. Ibid.
39. Ibid., 34-36.
40. Turpin, 163-65.
41. Ibid., 165.
42. Wood, 248.
43. "Intercourse, etc.," 42-44.
44. Ibid., 48.   Prince Damrong states Ayudhya was captured at night; See Prince Damrong, 341.
45. Wood, 249.
46. "Intercourse, etc.," 48.
47. Wood, 249.
48. Ibid.
49. "Intercourse, etc.," 53.

CHAPTER SIX

THE T'ONBURI PERIOD 1767 - 1782

The siege and capture of Ayudhya marks the final crest of Burmese military and political power in southeast Asia. Burma remained a great Asian power for about fifty years, and then declined largely as the result of a shortsighted and arrogant policy pursued by her kings until, finally, province after province was wrested from her imperial sway by British-Indian forces. The rump Kingdom of Burma was annexed to the British Empire in 1885.

> "As regards Siam, the fall of Ayudhya was a notable event indicating the period of the lowest depth of political decadence and military inefficiency into which it had gradually drifted, since the close of the glorious days of the famous King Pra Naresuan. Siam, on the other hand, did not remain low for long, but steadily rose in power, especially after the accession to the throne of the first King of the present dynasty [Rama I, 1782-1809], and by the dint of prowess in arms in the earlier periods, and by the adoption of a broad-minded and far-sighted policy in diplomacy in later periods, it has been able to maintain its independence up to the present day." [1]

Although several members of the old royal family of Siam survived the sack of Ayudhya, P'ya Taksin who was half Chinese by birth, alone furnished the leadership destined to free Siam from Burmese domination.[2] The great Thai patriot was assisted indirectly by the Chinese who waged war against the implacable Burmans during the years 1766-69. Four Chinese invasions were repulsed by the Burmese. King Hsinbyushin, however, was obliged to withdraw most of his troops from Siam for the protection of the Burmese homeland. The preoccupation of King Hsinbyushin with Chinese affairs precluded all thought of decisive Burmese intervention in Siam until the Chinese menace to Burma had been liquidated.[3]

When the main Burmese army left Ayudhya for Burma in June 1767, the Burmese general, Sugyi, remained with small Burmese forces to control Siam for King Hsinbyushin. He established a camp near the ruins of the old capital at a place called the Three Bo Trees.[4]

P'ya Taksin who had incurred the displeasure of King Boromoraja V had fled Ayudhya with five hundred followers before the Burmese conquest.* [5] Eluding Burmese pursuers P'ya Taksin established a base of operations at Rayong on the Gulf of Siam. When Ayudhya fell to the Burmese in April 1767, P'ya Taksin controlled both Rayong and Jonburi (Chonburi). He acquired Chantabun (Chanthaburi) in June 1767 and Trat shortly afterwards. By October P'ya Taksin controlled a large territory unravaged by the Burmese, and his success induced others to join his ranks.

---

* P'ya Taksin had fallen into disfavor because (1) he failed to assist a colleague during a sortie from the beleaguered capital, and (2) he fired a large cannon at the enemy without obtaining the sanction of the king who had forbidden the discharge of the larger artillery pieces without royal permission.

About the same month (October) P'ya Taksin, with an army of five thousand men and a flotilla of one hundred war canoes, ascended the Menam River and captured the city of T'onburi. The renegade Thai, Nai T'ong In, who ruled T'onburi for the Burmese, was executed for his labors.[6]

> "[General] Sugyi now sent a large army under one Maung Ya, to expel P'ya Taksin. Maung Ya's force was, however, partly composed of Siamese, who at once began to desert, and Maung Ya fled back to the camp of the Three Bo Trees. P'ya Taksin pursued him and attacked the Burmese camp, which was taken after a short but fierce fight. . . . This event marks the liberation of Siam from the Burmese, only six months after the capture and destruction of the capital."[7]

Although P'ya Taksin had planned to re-establish Ayudhya as the capital of Siam, he altered his design, returning to T'onburi where he was crowned king at the new capital.* To establish Ayudhya as the capital would have necessitated greater resources in men and money than King Taksin (1767-82) commanded. Moreover the king of T'onburi was not the only aspirant to the kingship in Siam—temporarily shattered by the mailed fist of King Hsinbyushin—since five different sovereigns ruled various parts of the old Ayudhyan kingdom during the early months of 1768. As yet no Thai king had established a hegemony of the resources of the old state including:

I. The king of T'onburi, Taksin, who controlled Siam of the Lower Menam.

II. The king of P'imai, T'ep P'ip'it, a son of Maha T'ammaraja II (1733-58), who ruled the eastern provinces including Korat.

III. The king of P'itsanulok, Ruang.

IV. The king of Fang (Utaradit), Ruan, a debauched Buddhist priest, who ruled a theocratic state with his capital at Sawangburi near Utaradit.

V. And the king of Nak'on Srit'ammarat (Ligor), Musika, who ruled most of peninsular Siam.

King Taksin was, therefore, only one of many rulers contending (in whole or in part) for the heritage of Boromoraja V.

Having repulsed the third Chinese invasion early in 1768, King Hsinbyushin ordered the governor of Tavoy to join forces with a Burmese army encamped at Ratburi. The Siamese, however, commanded by the king of T'onburi, were not the same flaccid warriors of recent years—the Ratburi camp and the entire Burmese fleet were captured by the Thais, and the governor of Tavoy driven from Siamese territory.

Encouraged by his success against the Burmese, King Taksin sought in May 1768 to encompass the ruin of King Ruang of P'itsanulok. Fate, however, decreed against the king of T'onburi and he suffered defeat. King Ruang, elated by his success, staged a coronation ceremony at which he was formally crowned king of Siam. Within a week he was dead. King Ruang was succeeded by a younger brother, P'ra In, who avoided the royal style of Siam. King P'ra In,

---

* T'onburi was the capital of King Taksin until his death in 1782.

103

however, was outmatched by the deft Priest-King Ruan who captured P'itsanulok in 1768 after a two month siege. The king of Fang (Utaradit) now emerged as the foremost rival of the king of T'onburi.

King Taksin further narrowed the field of possible contenders for the supreme kingship when he annexed the lands of the ephemeral Kingdom of P'imai at the close of the rainy season (1768). The king of P'imai fled, seeking asylum in the neighboring Kingdom of Vien Chang (Vientiane), but he was pursued and captured. King Taksin, until unbalanced by insanity, was not of an ungenerous nature. The king of T'onburi was prepared to offer the royal scion his life, but the insolence of T'ep P'ip'it forbade such a course and he was executed.[8]

As is often the case during a time of troubles, nature conspired with man to oppress the common people. Recently deluged by an inundation of insatiable Burman warriors, the Siamese in 1769 were also visited with a drought causing a great famine which the ravages of war aggravated. Destructive rodents devoured the rice in the fields, and swarms of insects waged war against the living and dead.[9]

> "Under these unhappy conditions Phya Tak [King Taksin] showed his generous spirit: The needy were destitute no longer. The public treasury was opened for the relief. In return for cash, foreigners supplied them with the products that the soil of the country had refused. The Usurper justified his claims by his benevolence. Abuses were reformed, the safety of property and persons was restored, but the greatest severity was shown to malefactors. Legal enactments at which no one complained were substituted for the arbitrary power that sooner or later is the cause of rebellions. By the assurance of public peace he was able to consolidate his position and no one who shared in the general prosperity could lay claim to the throne."[10]

The attempt of King Taksin to assert the ancient Siamese suzerainty in Cambodia miscarried in 1769 when a rumor that King Taksin was dead gained currency among the Thai generals sent to reduce Cambodia, and fearing disturbances at T'onburi, the Siamese commanders returned to Thailand after occupying Siemrap (Siem Reap) and Battambang.*

While Thai troops marched into Cambodia King Taksin dispatched an army to peninsular Siam. The southern force was defeated at Jaiya (Chaiya) by forces of the Ligor king, but King Taksin arriving by sea, led his quarreling generals to victory. The army of King Musika was routed (perhaps near Chaiya), and the king of Ligor fled to Nak'on Srit'ammarat (Ligor). His position, however, was hopeless and when King Taksin approached the city, Musika fled to Patani. The Rajah of Patani, threatened with immediate war, delivered his dangerous guest to King Taksin.[11] Although the king of T'onburi had councillors who urged the execution of the fallen Musika, the noble nature of King Taksin refused such a course.

---

* Moura in *Le Royaume du Cambodge* declares the Siamese army advanced as far as Angkor, but was defeated by the Cambodian army.

' "No, he [King Musika] was never my servant, nor I his master. We were both servants of King Ekat'at [Boromoraja V], and when our master was dead, neither of us had any better right than the other to set himself up as King. My luck has been better than his, that is all." ' [12]

The ex-king, Musika, eventually regained the governorship of Nak'on Srit'ammarat (Ligor), stripped of his kingly pretensions, but in the capacity he served Siam prior to the fall of Ayudhya.[13]

The five separate Thai sovereignties of immediate post-Ayudhya days in 1770 had been reduced to two: T'onburi and Fang (Utaradit), the latter ruled by the grisly priest-king, Ruan.

"The yellow robe worn by this abominable man was the only religious thing about him. His rule was a disgrace to humanity and an insult to the religion which he sacrilegiously professed to follow. He and his followers wallowed in blood and steeped themselves in drunkenness and vice." [14]

When Priest-King Ruan raided Chainat early in 1770, King Taksin moved to overthrow the Kingdom of Fang (Utaradit) and her reprobate king. Three armies, totaling twenty thousand men or more, invaded the northern kingdom. P'itsanulok was easily captured, and the T'onburi commander, P'ya Yomarat, proceeded, after a short delay, to besiege the stockaded capital, Sawangburi. King Ruan, unable to withstand the T'onburi forces, fled to the north. History, however, does not record the ultimate fate of the king of Fang (Utaradit). With the exception of Tavoy and Tenasserim, occupied by the Burmese, King Taksin had re-established the Kingdom of Siam within roughly the limits of the later Ayudhyan kingdom—a tribute to the resource, courage and perspicacity of the king of T'onburi.

Buddhist priests were dispatched by King Taksin to reform the Buddhist religion in the north. Those priests who could not pass the prescribed tests were expelled from the priesthood and punished.[15] Turpin states King Taksin especially hated priests (and there were many) who abused their powers by fomenting sedition among the untutored masses.[16]

About the time of the Fang (Utaradit) campaign King Taksin sought to annex Chiengmai but was repulsed by the Burmese.[17] The brave new world of King Taksin also witnessed a recrudescence of the old enmity with Cambodia, as well as the comparatively new competition with the Vietnamese for supremacy in Cambodia.

Following the Burmese capture of Ayudhya in 1767 two princes of the Thai royal family escaped to Hatien (in present-day Cambodia). They received the protection of Mac Thien-tu—the governor of Hatien for the Nguyen of Hue. In 1768 King Taksin asked Mac Thien-tu to return the princes offering the governor territory in exchange. Mac Thien-tu replied evasively and dispatched a fleet whose commander mediated treachery against King Taksin under the pretext of delivering a rice consignment. The plot failed and the commander of the fleet was imprisoned. When King Taksin attacked Ligor in 1769, Mac Thien-tu mistakenly divined the opportunity to recoup his losses had arrived. A large fleet was equipped, and an army of fifty thousand men disembarked on the coast of Siam. The army of Mac Thien-tu, however, remained immobilized for several months, and having accomplished nothing of consequence, returned to Hatien stricken with the plague.

After a victorious campaign in the Peninsula, King Taksin directed his armies against Mac Thien-tu and Prea Outey (1758-75), the king of Cambodia.* Mac Thien-tu retreated from Chau-doc, and King Prea Outey upon the approach of the Siamese fled without offering combat. King Taksin entered Phnom Penh placing the Siamese candidate, Ang Non, on the readily disposable Cambodian throne. But now the Nguyen of Hue intervened at the decisive moment. Vietnamese troops were dispatched from Khanh-hoa and other places. The bulk of the Vietnamese army apparently ascended the Mekong River, and a water-borne detachment occupied Rachgia on the Gulf of Siam. Maybon states a battle was fought at Phnom Penh in which the Annamites (Vietnamese) were victorious. The Nguyen candidate, Prea Outey, reascended the Cambodian throne, and King Taksin retired to Hatien and later to Siam. A Siamese garrison held Hatien while the candidate of the king of T'onburi, Ang Non, retreated to Kampot.

In 1773 Mac Thien-tu made offers of peace which were accepted by King Taksin who withdrew his troops from Hatien. Ang Non, however, had strong support for his claims, and Prea Outey despaired of securing his throne and abdicated in favor of Ang Non (1775-79). In 1776 King Ang Non beat off a Vietnamese attack.[18] The Cambodians presumably recognized the suzerainty of Siam during the reign of King Ang Non, since as we shall see, they assisted the Siamese in the war against the Kingdom of Vien Chang in 1778.

King Hsinbyushin, having sacked Ayudhya and flaunted the might of Imperial China (repulsing all assaults of the celestial armies) was yet desirous to enhance his martial renown by a renewed advance in Laos and the Kingdom of Siam. In 1771 when Vien Chang (Vientiane) was invaded by the forces of King Int'a Som (1727-76) of Luang Prabang, King Ong Boun (1760-78) requested the aid of Burma (his suzerain power).[19] King Hsinbyushin quickly dispatched five thousand men and delivered his Lao vassal from immediate peril by defeating the Luang Prabang troops on the plain of Muong-Kassy.[20] In 1774 King Int'a Som offered alliance to King Taksin who readily accepted.[21] The Burmese meanwhile were active in Thailand, but their attempts to capture P'ijai in 1772 and 1773 were repulsed by the Siamese.[22]

Finally when King Hsinbyushin received a report from King Ong Boun of Vien Chang that the Siamese were threatening his kingdom, the former decided to make a vigorous effort to overthrow the Kingdom of Siam. He dispatched Nemyo Thihapate (who commanded the northern forces at the siege of Ayudhya 1766-67) with five hundred horse and seven thousand men, comprising twenty-two regiments, to the aid of his vassal. Having secured the safety of Sandapuri (Vien Chang) and requisitioned forces from vassal states along the line of march, King Hsinbyushin ordered Nemyo Thihapate to invade Siam. Leaving

---

* Maybon in his *Histoire Moderne du Pays D'Annam* (1592-1820) wrongly states Ang Tong was king of Cambodia at this time. Moura, in *Le Royaume du Cambodge*; Dauphin-Meunier in his *Histoire du Cambodge* and Ghosh in *A History of Cambodia* confirm that Prea Outey was king of Cambodia in 1758-75 and not Ang Tong.

106

the Burmese capital * in March 1773 Nemyo Thihapate successfully marched to Sandapuri (Vien Chang). But the Burmese were now confronted with an ugly situation in Chiengmai. The Burmese governor, Thado Mindin (1769-75), quarreled with native officials about the respective privileges of the latter. Led by Paya Sapan (P'ya Chaban) a delegation of Chiengmai chiefs journeyed to Burma to place their case before King Hsinbyushin. The chiefs returned with an order from the king stating that Thado Mindin should govern only in accordance with ancient custom. No definition of "ancient custom" was tendered and the existing disputes continued. An altercation ensued between the governor's men and Paya Sapan (P'ya Chaban), and the latter fled to Sandapuri (Vien Chang) where he received the protection of Nemyo Thihapate.

When Nemyo Thihapate and his Burmese force returned to Zinme (Chiengmai) he ordered Paya Sapan (P'ya Chaban) and Kawila, the governor of Lagun (Lamp'ang), to march in the van of the Burmese army with their contingents for the invasion of Siam, but the Burmese governor quarreled with Nemyo Thihapate, the former insisting that the two Chiengmai chiefs would not serve the Burmese cause loyally, the latter stating the two nobles were needed to keep their contingents under control. When the Burmese governor, Thado Mindin, attempted to arrest Paya Sapan (P'ya Chaban) and Kawila, both nobles bolted and fled to Siam.[23]

Upon hearing the news of a Mon rebellion (1773), and the capture of Martaban by the rebels, King Taksin with the Siamese forces, marched northward in November 1774 with the intention of depriving Burma of her Chiengmai appendage. Arriving at Rahaeng, King Taksin heard unwanted tidings—the Mon revolt had been suppressed. Doubt as to the next step perplexed the mind of the great Thai king, but learning of the divisions and turmoil in Chiengmai, King Taksin resolved to pursue his original design and marched on Chiengmai.**

P'ya Chakri, the future Rama I (1782-1809), with the Siamese advance guard crossed the frontier. The Burmese were routed at their Lamp'ang camp, and Chiengmai besieged in January 1775. When the Burmese garrison fled, King Taksin entered Chiengmai in state on January 16th, 1775 amid the plaudits of the populace.

P'ya Chaban was installed as the prince of Chiengmai. The submission of the chiefs of P're and Nan to King Taksin followed, and thus after half a millennium of separate political existence the northern and southern Thai were joined in one united Kingdom of Thailand.[24]

The plans of King Hsinbyushin for the overthrow of Thai independence included not only a swordsman's thrust from Chiengmai, parried by King Taksin, but also a thrust (by the Three Pagodas Pass) toward the midsection of the Kingdom of T'onburi. The governor of Mottama (Martaban), Mingyi Kamani Sanda, had organized a force to co-operate with Nemyo Thihapate. The revolt of the disgruntled Mons, however, delayed the advance into Siam while many Mons, harried by the Burmese, fled to Thai territory. Finally King Hsin-

---

* Ava was the capital of Burma from 1766-83 replacing Shwebo, the capital of Alaungpaya.

** The size of the Siamese army in the Chiengmai expedition is variously estimated between twenty and fifty thousand men.

byushin, apprised of the various delays at Zinme (Chiengmai) and Mottama (Martaban), dispatched in November 1774 a force of sixty-one regiments, twenty-five hundred horse and thirty-five thousand men commanded by Wungyi Maha Thihathura * to invade Siam by way of Mottama (Martaban) and Tayaik (a narrow pass not far from Ratburi).

Wungyi Maha Thihathura was joined by a force comprising twelve regiments commanded by Min-ye Zeyakyaw. The total Burmese force which marched by the Three Pagodas route contained about forty thousand men. The two Burmese commanders, however, could not agree upon a concerted strategy to defeat the Siamese. A Thai detachment at Tayaik sought to lure the Burmese into an ambush. Finally Min-ye Zeyakyaw, attending rumors of the illness of King Hsinbyushin, returned with his troops to Mottama (Martaban). When a Burmese force of three thousand men, commanded by the Bo of Satpyagon, came in contact with Thai forces at Tayaik, the Siamese withdrew in accordance with preconcerted strategy.[25]

> "The Bo of Satpyagon, who was present at the capture of Ayudhya and whose experience it had been to route the Siamese at every encounter, was over-confident of success and under-estimated the strength of the enemy and the generalship of the leader [presumably King Taksin]. Failing to take necessary precautions, he pressed hard on the gradually retreating Siamese till he got to Sakadan [in the Ratburi district], when he and his 3,000 men were completely hemmed in by two forces concealed thereabouts, at a place devoid of water. Wungyi Maha Thihathura became aware of the plight of Bo, the result of his own want of foresight and the Bo's rashness born of over-confidence. He sent Min-ye Yannaung with only 4,000 men to rescue the entrapped troops, but this handful of men was of no avail against a force of 20,000 Siamese. The Bo and his men dug hard for water, but as they were located on a parched, barren ridge of a strip of high-ground, their energy was wasted, and water could not be obtained. Thirst rendered them quite weak and helpless and they fell into the hands of the Siamese." [26]

The Burmese force surrendered in April 1775. Wood states a small force of two thousand men, which had been plundering in the direction of Sup'an, managed to escape, incurring severe losses. Two inroads of Burmese forces in the Rahaeng area were also repulsed about the same time. The Burmese in the Rahaeng district were pursuing Mon refugees. Their principal enmity was, therefore, probably directed against the rebel Mons rather than the Siamese.[27]

The *Hmannan Yazawin Dawgyi* further states Wungyi Maha Thihathura and Min-ye Zeyakyaw were eventually reconciled, uniting to defeat the Siamese at Sakadan before the commencement of the rainy season (1775). The Burman army, however, was short of supplies with a large sick-roll. The Burmese com-

---

* Wungyi Maha Thihathura was the Burmese general who repulsed the fourth and final Chinese invasion of Burma in 1769 during the Burmese-Chinese war of 1766-69.

mand, therefore, decided to withdraw their forces to Mottama (Martaban) for the duration of the rainy season, and when the rains ceased, to attack Thailand by the Ywahaing (Rahaeng) route where the gathering of provisions was expected to be easier.[28] Thus failed the Burmese double pincer movement (from Chiengmai and Martaban) by which King Hsinbyushin moved to repeat the triumphs of 1767. But the vigor of the Thai resistance, the stalwart leadership of King Taksin and the divisions among the Burmese forces led to the overthrow of the plans of King Hsinbyushin and the consequent retreat of his forces.

The Burmese were not dismayed. In October 1775 Nemyo Thihapate * descending from Chiengsen (still in Burmese hands) occupied Chiengmai, but the advance of P'ya Chakri and P'ya Surasih, the Chakri's younger brother, obliged Nemyo Thihapate to evacuate Chiengmai and to retire on Chiengsen.

Still the Burmese pressed the attack. At the close of the rainy season (1775) Wungyi Maha Thihathura ** advanced into Siam with a large army intending to occupy the northern portions of the kingdom. The Burmese crossed the frontier at Melamao (not far from Me Sot) occupying Rahaeng, and in January 1776, gathering momentum, the Burmese defeated a large Thai army commanded by P'ya Surasih near Sukhothai. The Burmese occupied Sukhothai, the ancient capital, and then besieged P'itsanulok. The danger to Siam was real. King Taksin in person commanded an army for the relief of P'itsanulok, but the Burmese tide rolled on, engulfing P'itsanulok at the high tide of Burman success. The city was stoutly defended by General Chakri but threatened by famine, his force was obliged to retire about March 1776. He established his headquarters at P'etchabun (apparently in concert with King Taksin). However, the operative cause of the Siamese defeat, i.e., famine, joined forces with the Thais to menace the Burmese position. Finally the Burmese retreated, under orders of recall from a new king, Singu Min (1776-82), suffering harassment from Thai forces, until the frontier was crossed in August 1776.[29]

The eminent qualities of P'ya Chakri were recognized by Wungyi Maha Thihathura during the fighting at P'itsanulok. The Burmese general requested a personal meeting with the Thai general:

> "A truce was arranged and the two opposing armies were drawn up facing one another with the two commanders on horseback. After an exchange of presents, they approached each other half-way across the gap in the field. Maha Thihathura said the days were over when the Burmese could conquer the T'ais. After lauding the generalship of his opponent, the Burmese general prophesied that General Chakri had high qualities which would one day lead him to become king." [30]

A prophesy fulfilled six years later when General Chakri established the dynasty which reigns at Bangkok today.

King Hsinbyushin died in June 1776 at the age of thirty-nine.[31] Hsinbyushin remains an imposing name in Burmese history. His two greatest accomplishments: the conquest of Ayudhya and the repulse of the imperial armies

---

* Or the Bo Supla of Wood
** Or the Maha Sihasura of Wood

mark King Hsinbyushin as a great Asian as well as Burmese conqueror. His later defeats in Thailand do not detract from the brilliancy of his conquests tarnished, however, as his reputation stands by his cruel order to raze the city of Ayudhya.

King Singu Min, the son of Hsinbyushin, was possessed of an ambition less encompassing than his royal forebear. He made one attempt to regain Chiengmai, but the city—besieged by the Burmese—was relieved in September 1776 by a Thai army. After his defeat at Chiengmai, King Singu Min reigned in peace with his Siamese neighbors.[32]

> "P'ya Chaban, however, felt unable to carry on the government of Chiengmai any longer, so depleted and impoverished had the city become. He retired to Lamp'ang, followed by most of the inhabitants of Chiengmai, and for twenty years the once mighty capital of King Mengrai [Mangrai] was left as a lair for the beasts of the jungle."[33]

In 1777 the governor of Nangrong, in Korat province, rebelled and formed an alliance with the independent prince of Champasak, Chao O. A Siamese army commanded by P'ya Chakri captured and executed the rebel of Nangrong. A second army led by P'ya Surasih dealt the prince of Champasak the same justice. Apparently a large territory on the right bank of the Mekong, extending in the south to K'ong, was annexed to the Kingdom of T'onburi.[34]

About the time of the Champasak expedition evidences of insanity of King Taksin became manifest.

> "He imagined that he had discovered certain physical resemblances between himself and Buddha, and indulged in various other eccentricities. His temper also grew very fierce and suspicious. On one occasion he was roused to fury merely because his hair had been imperfectly dressed on a ceremonial occasion, and when his son, Prince In P'itak, ventured to say a word in defence of the offending servant, the unfortunate Prince was seized and most unmercifully flogged."[35]

When the Siamese annexed Champasak, P'ra Woh, a rebel of Vien Chang (Vientiane), submitted to Siam. P'ra Woh had previously fled to Champasak territory and established himself at Mot Deng (near Ubon). The king of Vien Chang, Ong Boun (1760-78), as soon as the Siamese army had withdrawn from his immediate proximity, attacked P'ra Woh, bagging and then executing his victim. King Taksin regarded such action as tantamount to war and dispatched an expedition to invade Vien Chang.[36] The invading force was commanded by General Chulalok (P'ya Chakri). Two important columns invaded the territory of Ong Boun, one a force of twenty thousand men by land, and the other a force of about ten thousand men—which included a Cambodian contingent—ascended the Mekong in canoes. The invaders easily overcame the Laotian detachments sent against them. The siege of Vientiane lasted for four months.* Ong Boun fled when the city fell to the Siamese.[37] And Luang Prabang, the northern neighbor, was reduced to a state of vassalage.**[38]

---

* Wood states the Siamese emulated the Burmese in acts of cruelty during this campaign.

** Vientiane was captured with the assistance of Luang Prabang forces.

Vien Chang (Vientiane) was placed under Siamese military rule for a period of four years. In 1782 the fugitive Ong Boun was permitted to return to Vien Chang, stripped of his regal investments which were bestowed on his eldest son, Chao Nan (1782-92), who ruled Vien Chang as a vassal of Siam.[39]

In 1779 King Ang Non of Cambodia was toppled from his throne by Mu, the governor of Bassac, with the assistance of a Vietnamese army commanded by General Do Thanh-Nhon. King Ang Non was executed, and the infant Ang Eng (1779-96) placed on the ancient Khmer throne with Mu as regent.[40] King Ang Eng was the puppet of the anti-Thai party in Cambodia, and the king of T'onburi resolved to force Cambodia to play the Siamese tune. In the early months of 1781, a Thai army commanded by P'ya Chakri and P'ya Surasih, numbering twenty thousand men, was dispatched to Cambodia. The regent fled to Saigon to seek Vietnamese aid. A Vietnamese army advanced to Phnom Penh, but before combat was joined P'ya Chakri decided to return to Siam as the madness of King Taksin had precipitated a rebellion.[41]

> "After the departure of the army for Cambodia, King Taksin's eccentricities had become more pronounced. He imagined that he was developing into a Buddha, and commanded the priests to pay him divine honours. Some, through fear, assented, but many refused. These, to the number of over five hundred, were cruelly flogged, and the head priests among them were degraded and imprisoned.
>
> "The laity suffered still more severely. . . . The King began to suspect everybody of carrying on illicit trade. As he accepted the sworn statement of a single person as conclusive evidence of this, a detestable band of informers soon grew up, who waxed rich on fines extorted from their victims. The latter were not only plundered, but often flogged to death. Burning people alive became a common event. . . . On every side were heard the lamentations of innocent victims, groaning under the insensate tyranny of a madman." [42]

The revolt against King Taksin erupted in March 1782. A rebel army led by P'ya Sank'aburi marched against the T'onburi king who on March 30th was besieged in his own palace. The king surrendered and was allowed to enter a monastery.[43] P'ya Chakri received tidings of these events from the governor of Korat. The latter was ordered to restore order at the capital.[44] P'ya Chakri arrived at Bangkok on April 20th, entering the city amid expressions of a jubilant populace. The principal officials paid General Chakri homage including the hesitant P'ya Sank'aburi who also aspired to the throne. The officers of state urged the execution of the ex-king to ensure the repose of the kingdom to which Chakri with reluctance, but to his shame, assented. King Taksin was executed as were P'ya Sank'aburi and his principal adherents.[45]

King Taksin was only forty-eight at the time of his death.[46] The glory of his reign is attested by the reunion of his country, the repulse of the Burmese and the expansion of Siam in the Lao country. King Taksin found Siam prostrate before the feet of the proud Burman conqueror. He raised a fallen nation and a defeated people to new respect, contending on equal terms with the warlike Burmese and bringing the Lao states of Vien Chang (Vientiane) and Luang

Prabang into the Siamese state orbit. At his death the Thai nation was once again a great expanding Asian power and like the Kingdom of Ayudhya resuming the Siamese *Drang nach Osten.*

BIBLIOGRAPHY

1. Chula, H.R.H. Prince. *Lords of Life*, Taplinger Publishing Co., Inc., New York, 1960.
2. Dauphin-Meunier, A. *Histoire du Cambodge*, Presses Universitaires de France, Paris, 1961.
3. Ghosh, Manomohan. *A History of Cambodia*, J. K. Gupta, Saigon, 1960.
4. Hall, D. G. E. *A History of South-East Asia*, MacMillan & Co., Ltd., London, and St. Martin's Press, New York, 1961.
5. "Intercourse between Burma and Siam, as Recorded in Hmannan Yazawindawgyi," *Journal of the Siam Society*, Vol. VI, Part 2, Bangkok, 1959.
6. Le Boulanger, Paul. *Histoire du Laos Français*, Paris, 1931.
7. Maybon, Charles B. *Histoire Moderne du Pays D'Annam (1592-1820)*, Typographie Plon-Nourrit et Cie, Paris, 1919.
8. Moura, J. *Le Royaume du Cambodge*, Vol. II, Paris, 1883.
9. Turpin, François Henri. *History of the Kingdom of Siam*, Printed under the auspices of the Committee of the Vajiranana National Library, Bangkok, 1908. English translation by Cartwright, B. O.
10. Wood, W. A. R. *A History of Siam*, The Siam Barnakich Press, Bangkok, 1933.

FOOTNOTES

1. "Intercourse, etc.," 69. The quote is not part of the translation of the *Hmannan Yazawin Dawgyi* but is taken from the introductory remarks of the translator.
2. Hall, 389, 390.
3. "Intercourse, etc.," 68.
4. Wood, 251.
5. Ibid., 248.
6. Ibid., 251, 252.
7. Ibid., 252.
8. Ibid., 253-56.
9. Turpin, 178.
10. Ibid., 178, 179.
11. Wood, 257, 258.
12. Ibid., 258.
13. Ibid., 254, 258.
14. Ibid., 256.
15. Ibid., 259.
16. Turpin, 177, 178.
17. Hall, 392.
18. Maybon, 129-32.
19. Hall, 392.
20. Le Boulanger, 154.

21. Ibid., 196, 197.
22. Hall, 392.
23. "Intercourse, etc.," 74-78. Wood states P'ya Chaban massacred the Burmese in his force. A general massacre of the Burmese also occurred at Lamp'ang; See Wood, 263.
24. Wood, 262-64.
25. "Intercourse, etc.," 78-83.
26. Ibid., 83, 84.
27. Wood, 264, 265.
28. "Intercourse, etc.," 85.
29. Wood, 265, 266.
30. Prince Chula, 75.
31. "Intercourse, etc.," 85, 86.
32. Wood, 266, 267.
33. Ibid.
34. Ibid., 267.
35. Ibid.
36. Ibid., 268.
37. Le Boulanger, 155, 156.
38. Hall, 384.
39. Ibid., 380.
40. Ibid., 367.
41. Wood, 269, 270.
42. Ibid.
43. Ibid., 270, 271.
44. Hall, 395.
45. Wood, 272.
46. Hall, 395.

CHAPTER SEVEN

THE BANGKOK PERIOD

THE REIGN OF KING RAMA I 1782 - 1809

The first king of the Chakri dynasty, Rama I, the supreme lord of Thailand, established his capital at Bangkok, opposite T'onburi, on the east bank of the Menam River.   During the reign of King Rama I the Burmese were repulsed, the religion and laws of the kingdom reformed and a line of monarchs founded who have continued to occupy the Thai throne until present day.   The lineal descendant of the first Chakri king, Rama IX or Bumipol Adulet (1946-), the present king of Thailand, reigns at Bangkok as a constitutional monarch where Rama I ruled with absolute sway.

Rama I was crowned the king of Siam in June 1782 at Bangkok. He was forty-five years of age. Bangkok, lying on the east bank of the Menam (Chao P'raya) River, was chosen as the site of the new capital for strategic reasons since the wide and deep Menam offered a natural moat against attack from the west.[1]

"The area chosen for the Royal Palace was the China Town of old Bangkok, ruled as was then the custom by a rich Chinese merchant with the noble rank of P'raya. With suitable compensation, he was asked to move the Chinese community to Sampeng which is still the main China Town of modern Bangkok. The vacant ground was first marked out with a wooden fence, and wooden pavilions richly appointed were put up quickly so that the new monarch could have an early and provisional coronation on the chosen site for the new palace and capital city."[2]

A swamp on the eastern face of Bangkok protected the city in the east. Work on the new capital commenced in earnest in 1783. A special temple within the precincts of the Royal Palace was built to house the Emerald Buddha captured at Vientiane in 1778.* The temple as well as a portion of the Royal Palace were completed in 1785, and the Emerald Buddha was transferred from T'onburi, in grand procession, to Bangkok during the same year. Other buildings—of a religious nature—arose during the reign of King Rama I, including the Wat Po and Wat Sutat.[3]

The reader will recall that the Kingdoms of Siam and Burma lived in peace following the failure of the Burmese siege of Chiengmai in September 1776. Peace endured for nearly ten years, when King Bodawpaya (1782-1819), a younger son of the illustrious Alaungpaya (1752-60), renewed the now familiar Burmese aggression in 1785.

The reign of Bodawpaya commenced in a blood bath in which all possible rivals, including Wungyi Maha Thihathura, the famed general in the Chinese war of Hsinbyushin (1763-76), were put to death.[4] In 1784-85 King Bodaw-

---

* The Emerald Buddha today forms one of the main tourist attractions of present-day Bangkok.

paya annexed the ancient Kingdom of Arakan to the Burmese Empire.* [5] King Bodawpaya probably thought the Kingdom of Siam could be conquered with equal facility. If so, he misjudged his enemy. Glory and plunder are perhaps assignable as final causes of the Burmese attack. The *Hmannan Yazawin Dawgyi*, however, has not condigned to enlighten us on the purpose of the renewed Burmese aggression.

By the summer of 1785 Burmese preparations for a large scale invasion of Siam neared completion. In July a force of ten regiments including one thousand horse and ten thousand men, commanded by Mingyi Mingaung Kyaw, were dispatched by sea to Byeik (Mergui). The Burmese commander received orders from King Bodawpaya to execute preparations in readiness for the march of His Burman Majesty via the Three Pagodas Pass. In September 1785 ten regiments were dispatched to Dawe (Tavoy) under the leadership of Nemyo Nawrata. A week later a third Burman column, led by Maha Uzana,** received orders to march to Zinme (Chiengmai) presumably from the Burmese capital, then located at Amarapura.*** The army of Maha Uzana included twenty-nine regiments consisting of three thousand horse and thirty thousand men. Numerous Shan chiefs were obliged to supply contingents. Other regiments assembled at Mottama (Martaban) preparatory to the invasion of Siam by the Three Pagodas Pass.[6]

> "Then on the 10th of waxing Tazaungmon 1147 (November A.D. 1785), King Bodawpaya left the capital with an army of 40 regiments containing 500 elephants 5,000 horse, and 50,000 men, under his own command. . . . The Maha Upayaza [Crown Prince] was left in charge of the capital. . . . He [King Bodawpaya] travelled by land and passed through Taung-ngu [Toungoo], Shwegyin and Sittaung. Wherever the army camped His Majesty was entertained with music and theatrical performances. In thirty-eight marches he reached Mottama [Martaban], on the 4th of waning Nadaw (December). He found that sufficient provisions had not been collected and stored up at the different stages along the route he was to march to Yodaya [****]. Mingyi Mingaung Kyaw, who had been ordered to do this

---

* The history of Arakan is obscure and largely mythical prior to the foundation of Mrohaung as the capital of the kingdom ca. 1433. The early dynasties were Indian, but about the ninth or tenth century, the Burmese began to settle in Arakan. Although at times tributary to Pagan, Pegu and Ava, the Arakan kings managed to maintain a relative independence until the last king, Thamada 1782-85, was deposed by King Bodawpaya and the kingdom annexed to Burma.

** Wungyi Thado Thiri Maha Uzana

*** The Burmese capital remained at Amarapura (1783-1823), shifted to Ava (1823-37), returned to Amarapura (1837-57) and was finally established at Mandalay (1857-85) prior to the British conquest in 1885.

**** In the present context Bangkok, the capital, should be understood as the terminus of the march, rather than Yodaya (Ayudhya), the old capital.

and who had gone on to Byeik [Mergui], was ordered to be brought back to him under arrest. His Majesty sent Wungyi Maha Thiri Thihathu from his army to take over the command of Mingyi Mingaung Kyaw. He then dispatched a detachment of six regiments with Nawrata Kyawgaung in command to march to Yodaya [Bangkok] via Ywahaing [Rahaeng]." [7]

King Bodawpaya was also delayed, as well as irked, by the languid pace his commanders set in transporting men, horses and elephants across the Thanlwin (Salween) River. The king, assembling his officers, threatened to burn them alive unless they executed their various commands with greater promptitude.[8] The despot of Burma, in a fit of rage hurled a spear into the assembly of his commanders, wounding one of the assistant staff officers. The display of royal ferocity had the desired effect, infusing the cowed officers with greater energy as: "The transportation of the elephants, horses, and men across the river was completed that very evening." The king of Burma, in his sanguinary temper, marched through the Three Pagodas Pass about the month of January 1786.[9]

King Rama I prepared and executed a vigorous defense scarcely designed to assuage the violent temper of his Burman adversary or restore a shattered equilibrium. The brother of the king of Siam, the Maha Uparat (formerly P'ya Surasih), enlisted about thirty thousand troops in an army which guarded the southern approaches to Siam at Karnburi (Kanburi). A second army was stationed at Nakorn Sawan (Nak'on Sawan) toward the north. King Rama I held twenty thousand men, clad in bright red uniforms, in general reserve eventually assisting his brother, the Uparat, repulse the invaders at Karnburi (Kanburi).* [10]

The Burmese, after defeating the Siamese in a two-day fight west of Kanburi, marched with an advance force of thirty-three thousand men to Kanburi, attacked a somewhat smaller force of Siamese but were repulsed. The Burmese pitched camp, assumed a defensive posture and awaited reinforcements. The commissariat arrangements, however, collapsed and the Burmese forces soon exhausted their provisions. They subsisted on edible yams and roots. King Bodawpaya marched with reinforcements to relieve the beleaguered Burmese force near Kanburi. But when his commissariat arrangements foundered, he despaired of realizing his immediate aim, or larger ambitions, and decided to terminate the campaign ca. February 1786, sending despatch riders to the Burmese columns operating on his flanks with orders to return to Burma.

The Kanburi force retired as best it could, but six thousand men were captured by the Siamese during the retreat. A broken host of Burman warriors finally recrossed the frontier.[11]

The four remaining Burmese columns which invaded Thailand encountered various (mostly adverse) fortunes. The Zinme (Chiengmai) column commanded by Maha Uzana occupied northern Thailand, but Thai opposition stiffened and the Burmese received orders of recall after which they retreated to

---

* The invading Burmese numbered about one hundred thousand men in five columns reaching from Chiengmai in the north to the Peninsula in the south. Aimed like so many daggers at Siam, the Burmese encountered Thai forces also aggregating about one hundred thousand men.

Burma. The Ywahaing (Rahaeng) column led by Nawrata Kyawgaung after crossing the border and capturing Ywahaing (Rahaeng) was also recalled.[12]

The Burmese occupied part of peninsular Siam,[13] but in March 1786 the Maha Uparat was dispatched to clear the Burmese from the Peninsula—a mission he successfully accomplished.[14] A Burmese force, equipped with a flotilla, also attacked the island of Junk Ceylon. The Burmese invested the town of Chalang, but resistance was directed by a certain Lady Chan, the widow of the late governor, who bravely led numerous sorties against the besiegers forcing their withdrawal after a siege of one month. The Burmese raised the siege of Chalang in January 1786.[15]

Although the war machine of King Bodawpaya had run aground on the abrasive soil of Thai resistance, the king of Burma was not for that reason ready to forego preconceived tenets of aggression, or advance a good neighbor policy. Late in the year 1786 King Bodawpaya ordered a second invasion of the Kingdom of Siam with an army of fifty thousand men. Commanded by Mingyi Nanda Kyawdin * the Burman army marching by the route of King Bodawpaya, crossed swords with the Uparat of Siam, apparently near the Three Pagodas Pass, and unable to withstand the repeated Thai onslaughts the invaders were obliged to retire on Mottama (Martaban).** [16]

The Siamese in 1787 assumed the offensive attempting to wrench the one-time Ayudhyan province of Tavoy from the crown of Burma, but the siege of the city failed and King Rama I retreated. In the same year the Burmese were expelled from Chiengsen [17] which, in some measure, compensated for the Thai defeat in the south.

King Rama I made a final effort in 1792 to capture Tavoy. A quarrel between the governors of Dawe (Tavoy) and Mottama (Martaban) opened a cleavage for mischief followed, in due order, by a Siamese army which quickly occupied Dawe (Tavoy). King Rama I attempted the defense of the city (against the Burmese) with fifty thousand men while detailing the Maha Uparat to invest Byeik (Mergui) with twenty thousand men. King Bodawpaya unable to satiate his own extraterritorial ambitions, was able, at least, to quash designs of a foreign ruler against the integrity of the Burman kingdom. The upshot being that the Siamese were driven from Dawe (Tavoy) by the somewhat smaller forces of the Maha Upayaza—who seems to have sat out the campaign at Rangoon—in January 1793. The Uparat, attacked at Byeik (Mergui) by a Burmese relief column, made a precipitate retreat.[18] The attempt of King Rama I to occupy Tavoy and Mergui in 1792-93 was the last Thai attempt to sever, by armed force, the Burmese provinces of the Kra Peninsula from the crown of Burma.

While the kings of Burma and Siam were exhausting their strength in a mutual strife Great Britain and France were taking the first tentative steps leading to their establishment as territorial powers in southeast Asia during the nineteenth century. It would be unfair to state the two great powers of the west were acting on a preconceived plan to overthrow the independence of those southeast Asian states eventually attached to their respective colonial empires. Yet in time

---

* Siamese history states the Burmese Crown Prince.
** The size of the Thai army is not given in the Burmese *Hmannan Yazawin Dawgyi.*

the ambitions of the western powers waxed while the weakness of the indigenous states, their refusal to modernize their respective state systems and a not unusual haughty disdain of the native ruler for his western adversary, invited the imposition of colonial rule which has not been lifted until our own day.

In August 1786 Francis Light occupied the island of Penang, off the west coast of Malaya, as a factory sight for the British East India Company with the consent of the sultan of Kedah.* The sultan of Kedah was anxious to obtain British protection against his own suzerain, the king of Siam. While the sultan thought he had secured a British commitment to protect him against Siamese attack, and ceded the island to the East India Company with that belief in mind, no written engagement had been made by the British to defend Kedah. "The East India Company was not legally wrong, because it broke no agreement or promise, but it was morally wrong for holding on to Penang on terms which never, as they stood, satisfied the Sultan." [19]

"After five years the Sultan gave up hope of any further assurances by the Company, and prepared to take Penang by force. A war fleet was assembled at Prai, but Light, who knew well enough what was happening, attacked first and scattered the invasion force. The sultan now agreed to sign a treaty [1791] ceding the island of Penang to the East India Company in return for an annual payment to him and his successors of 6,000 Spanish dollars a year." [20]

In 1800 the sultan of Kedah further ceded to the British company a strip of land opposite Penang Island, renamed by the British Province Wellesley, receiving in return an increased annuity (10,000 dollars per year) from the British company.[21] The Siamese of course were less than pleased with the sultan of Kedah for the alienation of territory which they claimed in vassalage. Eventually British-Thai competition for influence in the Malay Peninsula engendered friction causing a flurry of diplomatic activity on both sides during the 1820s.

During the last quarter of the eighteenth century a civil war convulsed Vietnam. The Nguyen of Hue were threatened with deposition, but Nguyen Anh after many defeats (he was a refugee in Siam for a number of years) overcame the rebels, and in July 1802 annexed the formerly independent Tongking.** In June 1802 Nguyen Anh was proclaimed the emperor of Vietnam with the style of Gia-Long (1802-20). Nguyen Anh was assisted in his enterprise of Vietnam by the French missionary, Pierre Joseph Georges Pigneau de Behaine, with whom he formed a close friendship. Pigneau de Behaine, in support of the Nguyen, was able to raise money in France, and at Pondicherry (in India) he enlisted several hundred volunteers for service in Vietnam. French assistance was an important factor in helping Nguyen Anh to reunite Vietnam after more than a two hundred year division into separate Nguyen and Trinh spheres of influence.[22]

Although French political influence lapsed for many years after the reunification of Vietnam in 1802, the French missionary influence remained strong. The

---

* Abdullah, 1760-98.
** Ruled by the Trinh family 1592-1788 and by the Tayson family 1788-1802.

periodic persecutions of Christians in Vietnam following the death of the Emperor Gia-Long in 1820, induced the French to intervene at intervals on behalf of the Christian coreligionists. Finally in 1859 the French occupied Saigon—the first overt move in their establishment of a territorial dominion which in time embraced Cambodia, Laos (Vien Chang and Luang Prabang) as well as Vietnam.[23]

Having briefly reviewed the course of oriental history touching the initial establishment of European territorial possessions in Malaya and Vietnam, we resume our narrative of the reign of King Rama I, relating how the king aggrandized Siam, at the expense of Cambodia, while placing the Thai protege, King Ang Eng, on the often abused throne of the ancient Khmers. In 1794 King Rama I crowned King Ang Eng (1779-96)—who for many years had lived as a fugitive or in hiding—as the Thai vassal king of Cambodia, sending him to Cambodia in May 1794 with a Siamese army commanded by Ben, a Cambodian and the governor of Battambang province. The governor of Battambang acted on orders of the king of Siam who enjoined him to sever his political connection with Cambodia and serve in subjugation to the rule of Siam (as governor of Battambang). The governor of Angkor province was placed under the authority of Ben, and therefore subject to direction from Bangkok. Perhaps in this instance a verbal accord had been reached by the two sovereigns as to the consideration for the Siamese assistance. No trace of a written accord or convention remains. However a more probable explanation is that King Rama I and Ben (for valuable consideration) combined to despoil King Ang Eng of the western portion of his kingdom. Cambodian history belabors the crimes, intrigues and ambition of the infamous Ben leading us to believe he readily preferred personal gain to loyal service of King Ang Eng and the Kingdom of Cambodia.

The finest relics of the ancient Khmers, the temples of Angkor, passed under Thai dominion. The Siamese annexation of Battambang and Angkor was yet a further instance of the expansion of the Thais at the expense of the weaker Cambodian neighbor; an expansion which now threatened the Cambodian state with extinction—an extinction perhaps averted only by the imposition of French colonialism in the 1860s. Ben for his part discharged his command with efficiency, placed King Ang Eng in possession of his kingdom, pacified the troubled land and entered into possession of the province of Battambang in the service of the king of Siam.[24]

The Burmese in 1797-98 again attacked Thailand, but the drama of the earlier Thai-Burman wars has departed as the Burmese aimed for local success rather than the overthrow of Thai independence as in former years. The Burmese invaded Chiengmai, but were repulsed by the forces of the Maha Uparat.[25] Then:

> "In 1802 the Burmese made their last bid for Chiengmai
> and came right up to the city walls. Prince Kawila [prince of
> Chiengmai since 1796], and the men into whom he had in-
> stilled his own sense of patriotism for the House of Chakri,
> hotly defended their newly acquired city [resettled in 1796].
> The Burmese closely besieged them on all sides but they held
> out, and both sides were still fighting when the relieving army

arrived under the Uparaja [Uparat]. Unfortunately he was seriously ill with prostate trouble and unable to direct operations with his usual vigour, and the King sent the Deputy Uparaja [the nephew of King Rama I] to help him. The Burmese now formed themselves into a ring of camps, all around Chiengmai, which the T'ais in turn besieged and intended to take all of them by simultaneous assault. An order was issued to all ranks that the assaults had to succeed that night, and that they would all have breakfast inside Chiengmai. During the night the Burmese, having dug themselves in trenches outside their camps, put up a hot barrage of fire, but the assaults were all successful and Chiengmai was relieved. The T'ai army, with Prince Kawila's troops, and the army of the Prince of Vientiane [*], which had just arrived, followed the enemy in pursuit and drove them out of the kingdom of Rama I, which was from that time free [for all purposes] of the Burmese for the rest of his reign." ** [26]

In November 1803 the Maha Uparat, the former P'ya Surasih, and brother of King Rama I died at the age of sixty.[27] He had been a worthy companion in arms of the founder of the present dynasty, assisting his brother in repelling the Burmese and helping him aggrandize the Kingdom of Siam on the eastern marches. Shortly after the death of the Uparat his two sons, Princes Lamuan and Intapat, were convicted of plotting treason and executed. Before his death the Uparat had lamented the fact that neither son could inherit his office, and both sons were apparently preparing to seize the Palace of the Front if not the Royal Palace itself when the plot was uncovered. King Rama I discovered the Uparat was implicated in the plot.[28]

"The knowledge that the attempt[ed revolt] was supported by his brother hurt the King most deeply, and when it was time for the cremation in 1804, at first he would not attend, as his brother had loved his own family more than the State. But as always he accepted the wise counsel of his great officers, and he presided in person at the cremation which was arranged as a very great State occasion." [29]

The Siamese supremacy in Cambodia, established in 1794, was shortly afterward challenged by the reunited Vietnam of Gia-Long (1802-20). King Ang Chan (1802-34) was appointed king of Cambodia, following the death of Ang Eng (1779-96) and a six year interregnum. The eleven year old king received

---

* The reader will recall that Chao Nan was invested by the Siamese with the governorship of Vien Chang (Vientiane) in 1782. In 1791 he attacked Luang Prabang (reduced to vassalage by the Siamese in 1778) and captured the city. However, King Rama I disapproved of the forward policy of his prince-vassal, and deposed Chao Nan in 1792, substituting his brother, Chao In 1792-1805, on the throne of Vien Chang (Vientiane). Prince Chao In ruled as a loyal vassal of Siam, and is the Prince of Vientiane mentioned above.

** Actually the Burmese raided Junk Ceylon in August 1809 before the death of King Rama I in September of the same year.

formal sanction from Siam for his ascent to the throne. His advisers, mindful of previous struggles in Cambodia between the Thais and Vietnamese for supremacy, sought to maintain friendly relations with the courts of Bangkok and Hue, and paid tribute to both. In 1805 King Ang Chan petitioned Gia-Long for leave to render annual homage to the Empire of Vietnam. To such ready obeisance the Emperor Gia-Long could offer no counter and granted King Ang Chan his request. The Cambodians, however, were unwilling to antagonize the Thai court, and in 1806 King Ang Chan journeyed to Bangkok for his coronation ceremony.[30]

> "This did not prevent him from sending a mission to Hue in the following year bearing tribute and requesting investiture as a vassal of Gia-Long. The emperor at once responded by sending him an embassy bearing the book of investiture together with a seal of gilded silver surmounted by a lion. This evoked a further mission in 1808 from Cambodia with thanks for the investiture thus accorded. Hardly a year went by without a mission between the two Courts. So things might have continued had it not been for the inevitable family squabble which offered the ever-watchful Siam the longed-for opportunity to intervene." [31]

In 1812 Ang Snguon rebelled against his brother, King Ang Chan, but we defer discussion of the revolt, and the subsequent Thai involvement in Cambodian affairs, while engaging the reader's attention in brief review of the domestic reforms of King Rama I. The reconstruction of the Kingdom of Siam after years of interminable war with Burma demanded the particular care of Rama I, the Lord of Life and absolute master of all subject to his imperious sway. As the Burmese threat to the independence of Thailand receded in the years following 1786, King Rama I was able to institute reforms in the Thai Buddhist church and legal system. In the religious sphere King Rama I reorganized the Buddhist hierarchy, summoned a church council in 1788 to revise certain canonical misconstructions in the Thai version of the "Tripitaka," or Buddhist scriptures, and unfrocked profligate monks. The laws of the Thai kingdom were reformed in the Law Code of 1805-08. Reformation of the legal system was especially necessary in the prevailing legal confusion following the Burmese sack of Ayudhya in 1767, when nine-tenths of the written legislation of Siam was destroyed in the flames of the old capital. However, no drastic legal revision was attempted. King Rama I was content to search the past texts and records, such as had survived, to ascertain the wisdom of his ancestors where possible and bring the modern into conformity with the ancient where practical.[32]

Prince Chula (in his book *Lords of Life*) offers an interesting glimpse of the daily routine of a Siamese monarch during the period before the renewal of sustained western contacts. For instance a normal day in the life of King Rama I began with an early rising and the distribution of food to the monks with their bowls. At 11:30 A.M. the king heard a report of the treasury expenses, following which he ascended the throne and gave audience first to members of the royal family, and then to various officers of the government, after which King Rama I lunched alone and then took an afternoon rest. At 6 P.M. the king partook supper. Then he heard a sermon. Later in the evening King Rama I

121

held evening audience at which he received reports about provincial matters. His business day usually closed at 9 or 10 P.M. but on rare occasions extended later in the evening. King Rama I followed a regular routine until 1807 when he became ill and infirm. Two years later (September 7, 1809) the first king of the Chakri dynasty died at the age of seventy-two.[33]

We do not fail to herald the merits of King Rama I. The repulse of the Burmese and Thai expansion on the Cambodian frontier attest the success of his military strategy. The legal and religious reforms of King Rama I bear testimony to his concern for the welfare of his subjects and kingdom. Taksin, Surasih and Rama I (as king and P'ya Chakri) guided the Thai ship of state through the tempest of successive Burman inundations sharing the glory and labor of securing the independence of Siam, as well as aggrandizement of the Thais. Nevertheless we dare not accord King Rama I a rank with the greatest of Siamese monarchs of the past. Lacking the personableness of Rama Khamheng (1275-1317), the creativity of Trailok (1448-88) or the commanding presence of Naresuen (1590-1605), King Rama I ruled a state which in the eighteenth and nineteenth centuries compared unfavorably with thirteenth, fifteenth or sixteenth century Siam in relative material strength. Although the Kingdom of Siam acquired the ascendency among the indigenous states of southeast Asia during the nineteenth century, yet the position of the Thai kingdom in the wider world beyond her borders had sadly deteriorated. Ensconced in semi-seclusion, Thai society was by-passed by the industrial revolution transforming the societies of Europe and America. Her industrial and administrative techniques would show how woefully defective her state system was in international rivalry with the states of the west in the nineteenth century. Nor was the Thai state system designed to enlist a response in the chord of Thai hearts until the Indianized state system, which denied the common man participation in national life, was overthrown and a more equitable system substituted.

The Siamese state ruled by Rama Khamheng, Trailok and Naresuen compared not unfavorably in material civilization with the nations of the west which, by the nineteenth century, had far outdistanced Siam in the productive techniques of civilized life. Nor was the Siamese kingdom, prior to the seventeenth century, inferior to the nations of Europe in military prowess. We are reminded of the power of King Bayinnaung (1551-81), the great Burman conqueror and adversary of the Thais, by the sixteenth century Venetian merchant-adventurer, Caesar Frederick, who was amazed that in the Burmese army:

> ". . . there should be such goodly orders . . . which be distinct in squares of Elephants, of horsemen, of harquebushers and pikemen, that truly the number of them are infinite: . . . his [Bayinnaung's] harquebushers are most excellent, and alway in his warres he hath eightie thousand harquebushes, and the number of them encreaseth dayly. Because the king will have them shoote every day at the Plancke, and so by continuall exercise they become most excellent shot: also hee hath great Ordinance made of very good mettall; to conclude there is not a King on the earth that hath more power or strength then this king of Pegu. . . ."[34]

Yet the armies of King Nanda Bayin (1581-99), the son of Bayinnaung, were unable to defeat, in sanguinary struggle, the Siam of King Naresuen. The conclusion we draw is that the Kingdom of Siam in the sixteenth century was one of the great powers of the world. The backward kingdom of Rama I, however, was no longer a state of great power stature.

King Rama I was content to exercise his statecraft within the context of the old Ayudhyan state system, perhaps, suitable for Thai needs in the days of Trailok and Naresuen but strangely anachronistic in the approaching world society of the nineteenth century.

The king of Siam as an individual poses as a man of industrious, regular and workmanlike habits, judged by the environment in which he lived; a competent general, but not overly scrupulous—the execution of Taksin reflects discredit on his reign and Rama I conducted the Lao campaign of 1778 (while still P'ya Chakri) with unbecoming ferocity. Yet, appraising his reign within the system in which he ruled, King Rama I deserves our respect as the monarch who defeated the last of the great Burmese invasions directed against the Kingdom of Siam.

BIBLIOGRAPHY

1. Chula, H.R.H. Prince. *Lords of Life*, Taplinger Publishing Co., Inc., New York, 1960.
2. Gerini, G. E. "Historical Retrospect of Junkceylon Island," *Journal of the Siam Society*, Vol. II, Part 2, Bangkok, 1905.
3. Hakluyt, Richard. *Voyages*, Vol. III, Everyman's Library, London, 1962.
4. Hall, D. G. E. *A History of South-East Asia*, MacMillan & Co., Ltd., London, and St. Martin's Press, New York, 1961.
5. "Intercourse between Burma and Siam, as Recorded in Hmannan Yazawindawgyi," *Journal of the Siam Society*, Vol. XIII, Part 1, Bangkok, 1919.
6. Kennedy, J. *A History of Malaya* A.D. 1400-1959, St. Martin's Press, 1962.
7. Moura, J. *Le Royaume du Cambodge*, Vol. II, Paris, 1883.

FOOTNOTES

1. Prince Chula, 79, 80.
2. Ibid., 80.
3. Ibid., 90-93.
4. "Intercourse, etc.," 1.
5. Ibid., 4, 5.
6. Ibid., 7, 8.
7. Ibid., 8.
8. Ibid., 8, 9.
9. Ibid., 11, 12.
10. Prince Chula, 97-99.
11. "Intercourse, etc.," 15-17.
12. Ibid., 17, 18.
13. Ibid., 18, 19.
14. Gerini, 61.
15. Ibid., 59, 60.

16. "Intercourse, etc.," 19-21. Prince Chula indicates the Siamese gained the victory near Karnburi (Kanburi); See Prince Chula, 100.
17. Prince Chula, 100-02.
18. "Intercourse, etc.," 39-51.
19. Kennedy, 77, 78.
20. Ibid., 79.
21. Ibid.
22. Hall, 366-71.
23. Ibid., 556-60.
24. Moura, 98, 99.
25. Prince Chula, 102.
26. Ibid., 102, 103.
27. Ibid., 111.
28. Ibid.
29. Ibid., 111, 112.
30. Hall, 373.
31. Ibid., 373, 374.
32. Prince Chula, 85-90.
33. Ibid., 113, 114.
34. Hakluyt, 248.

CHAPTER EIGHT

THE BANGKOK PERIOD
The Reign of King Rama II 1809 - 1824

King Rama II, the eldest son of Rama I, ascended the throne of Siam at the age of forty-one, having, in 1807, been appointed to the office of the Maha Uparat.[1] He was immediately faced with a threatening situation in peninsular Siam. The Burmese in August 1809, shortly before the death of King Rama I, equipped a flotilla, attacked, and plundered the island of Junk Ceylon, before returning to Tavoy in the same month (or soon thereafter). The rear division of the Burmese flotilla, however, encountered a storm near Thalang and was captured by the Siamese.

In November 1809 a second Burmese expedition attacked Junk Ceylon raiding Takua-pa and Takua-thung on the way. The Siamese dispatched reinforcements, totaling between ten and twenty thousand men, via Chaiya and Ligor to effect the relief of the island. The Thai column based on Ligor, commanded by P'ya Yomaraj (Yomarat), crossed the Peninsula to Trang where P'ya Thai-nam, with a force in thirty boats, advanced to Junk Ceylon from the south. The accidental explosion of a barrel of gunpowder threw the Thai ranks into confusion as P'ya Thai-nam and forces were preparing to land near Phuket on Junk Ceylon. P'ya Thai-nam was killed and several vessels destroyed. The Burmese captured Phuket and Thalang in January 1810, pillaged the island, and returned to Tavoy before the Thai Chaiya and Ligor forces could offer assistance.

Finally we relate the last Burmese attack on Junk Ceylon, hardly worthy of cognizance by reason of the paucity of force employed and the pettiness of aim, yet remarkable as the last Burmese invasion of the Kingdom of Siam. The Burmese, however, continued to threaten Thailand until they were overwhelmed by the British in the First Anglo-Burmese War 1824-26. As to the Burmese attack on Junk Ceylon, we merely relate that in December 1811 or January 1812 five thousand Burmese besieged Thalang, but were repulsed by the local inhabitants. The Burmese returned to their native land never again to tarry in arms upon the soil of Thailand.[2]

In Chapter VII we briefly mentioned the revolt of Ang Snguon of Cambodia, but deferred discussion for a later occasion. We now, however, resume our narrative with a discussion of Thai involvement (anew) in Cambodian affairs.

Ang Snguon, the brother of King Ang Chan (1802-34) of Cambodia, wished to be named Second King (and govern part of the kingdom). Rebuffed by his brother, Ang Snguon appealed to King Rama II to support his pretensions. The king of Siam was not adverse to meddling in troubled eastern waters, dispatching an army to Cambodia in support of Ang Snguon. King Ang Chan fled to Vietnam, and the Siamese occupied Oudong. In 1813 a Vietnamese army intervened in the Cambodian struggle, and the Siamese retired to Battambang without resisting the Vietnamese advance. Ang Chan remounted his unsteady throne and Ang Snguon, his brother, retired to Siam where he died in 1822.[3]

King Ang Chan, however, was not so easily rid of the Siamese. In 1814 Thai forces marched into northern Cambodia and occupied the provinces between

Angkor and Stung Treng.[4] Sandwiched between the ambitions of her larger neighbors—Siam and Vietnam—the Kingdom of Cambodia was slowly being devoured. During the 1830s the Vietnamese attempted to absorb the rest of Cambodia, but without success. In 1845 the Thai and Vietnamese governments agreed to establish a joint protectorate in Cambodia. Finally in the 1860s the French established their dominion in the Kingdom of Cambodia, and in time, regained for the ancient Khmer kingdom the provinces of Battambang and Angkor as well as the provinces lost to King Rama II in 1814.

The Kingdom of Siam from the days of King P'etraja (1688-1703) had increasingly lived divorced of contacts with the nations of the west. The Dutch with difficulty maintained a factory at Ayudhya until 1767, and the French continued their missionary activities but with little success. The Siamese were suspicious of the turbulent westerners, who threatened to overthrow the established order in southeast Asia, and the latter were preoccupied with their respective struggles in Europe, India and the East Indies. The renewal of the Burmese wars commencing with Alaungpaya's (1752-60) invasion of Siam in 1760 impeded commercial intercourse with the west, and the preferential treatment meted to Chinese merchants, who were considered politically innocuous in those bygone days, further discouraged western intercourse with the Kingdom of Siam. Nevertheless what we might call a Siamese wall of seclusion, fashioned of Thai mistrust and western disinterest, commenced to crumble during the reign of King Rama II. The termination of the Napoleonic wars (1793-1815) and the War of 1812 (1812-14) herald the beginning of a new age of commercial and political intercourse between the nations of the western world (including the United States) and the Kingdom of Siam. Although western interest in Siam was partly reanimated, Thai suspicion of western activity continued, and the final breach in the wall of seclusion did not occur until the reign of Rama IV (1851-68). Yet the first overt move to re-establish contacts with a western nation was made during the reign of King Rama II who allowed the Portuguese to establish a consulate at Bangkok.

After preliminary communication with the court of Bangkok the Portuguese dispatched the following letter to King Rama II:

LETTER FROM THE VICEROY OF GOA TO THE KING OF SIAM

"Magnificent, Powerful and Honored King of Siam.

"I, Diogo de Souza, Count of Rio Pardo, State Counselor of His Venerable Majesty, Vice-King and General Chief-of-Staff for all the States of India for His Highness and Powerful King of the United Kingdom of Portugal, Brazil and Algarves, My Master and Venerable Brother of Your Majesty having Learned of your dispatch through correspondence with your Cabinet Ministers that Your Highness was willing and had the sincere desire to establish with the Portuguese Nation the same old Peace, true alliance and reciprocal interests of commerce which existed in times passed, I hastened in advising the Counselor Secretary of this Magnificent [Portuguese] State to prepare a Preliminary [Commercial Treaty] of Twenty-three articles that may serve as basis for a Later Treaty which will be presented to Your Majesty through the

dispatch of the Secretary of Foreign Affairs [the P'rak'lang?]
and I would greatly appreciate that should Your Majesty find
them in accordance with the principles of true justice to give
them as soon as possible Your Royal Approval in order that
they may become effective without delay within your expanded Domains.

"Being convinced that the moving into the Court of Carlos
Manoel da Silveira would be agreeable to Your Majesty, I
appointed him as Consul General and Mandate of the Portuguese Nation in Your Majesty's Domains; with these thoughts
I hope that Your Majesty will see it fit that his personal values
[qualifications?] may receive recognition and that he will be
given all due Privileges. Also I hope that Your Majesty will
permit that he may bring unto your Presence some small gifts
listed on the Secretary Counselor's Note of this Magnificent
State addressed to the Minister of the Department, gifts which
show my gratitude and which were meant for the High Dig-
nity of Your Majesty, for the Queen your Wife and for the
Prince your presumptive Successor.

"May God Preserve the Person of Your Majesty." [5]

Goa the 30th of April 1820.
The Count of Rio Pardo.

The Thai court inserted clauses in the preliminary treaty to which the
Portuguese objected, and the treaty was never ratified by the Goan authorities.[6]
Nevertheless Da Silveira, a native of Brazil, was installed as Consul in 1820,
and received a small piece of land from the Thai government on which to con-
struct a factory. The Portuguese consul was a man of learning, speaking both
the English and French languages with fluency.[7] Still his cultural attainments did
not secure his person the inviolability usually accorded the emissaries of sovereign
nations. John Crawfurd, who headed the British embassy to Siam in 1822,
relates Consul Da Silveira on one occasion was arrested and threatened by the
Siamese with bastinado. "The personal treatment pursued towards the Consul
is such as if observed towards a British Agent must bring on a war in less than
six months." [8] Why the Portuguese labored under such disabilities is not clear,
since their commercial intercourse with the kingdom was of a limited nature.

The American trade with the Kingdom of Siam commenced in the year
1818 with the arrival of a solitary merchant ship. Three ships followed in 1819
and four ships in 1821. However the American trade was subject to the same
vexations as European trade with the kingdom,[9] including days if not weeks of
delay in the disposal of cargoes.

John Crawfurd — 1823

"The Americans with all the prudence and discretion which
mark these people as traders, do not seem to have fared better
than others. They [however] have received, I was informed
at Siam, a promise to be allowed to establish a Consul-ship at
Bangkok, but of this permission they have not availed themselves. . . ." [10]

The promise of a consulship was perhaps in deference to the nature of the American trade which included the merchandise of firearms readily demanded by the Thais,[11] but their western affiliations—and the imputation of intent applicable to Europeans—were spectres which haunted the American as well as European merchant in his relationship with the Siamese.

The Dutch also sought to renew the old intercourse with Siam, and dispatched an agent to Bangkok in 1820. The Dutch mission, however, was a complete failure, and the conduct of the Siamese court was both illiberal and irritating to the envoy.[12]

Although the first cracks in the Siamese wall of seclusion are discernible in the reign of King Rama II yet they are not very wide, and as we shall later see a further assault on the wall by a representative of the supreme government of India (John Crawfurd) failed to secure a relaxation of the restrictions which impeded British-Indian commerce with the Kingdom of Siam.

The Siamese during the reign of King Rama II commenced a vigorous forward movement in the Malayan Peninsula as indeed the Thais had pursued on the Cambodian frontier since the days of Sri Indraditya (1238-75) and Rama Khamheng (1275-1317). The application of Thai power in the Peninsula bore heavily on the tributary sultanate of Kedah. In November 1816 the court of Bangkok ordered Sultan Ahmad Taju'd-din (1798-1821) of Kedah to invade and subdue the independent state of Perak. The sultan of Kedah reluctantly complied with the Siamese demand, as he had no quarrel with his southern neighbor. Sultan Abdu'l-Malik Mansur Shah (1806-25) of Perak requested the intervention of the British East India Company but to no purpose. The Kedah forces required two years to reduce Perak, and on November 18, 1818 the Sultan Abdu'l-Malik Mansur Shah reported to Penang the conquest of Perak. In June 1819 the sultan of Kedah was busily attending the dispatch of Perak's tribute (Bunga Mas) to Siam.[13]

The demands placed on the sultan of Kedah by his Thai suzerain yearly became more burdensome. In 1818, before the completion of the sultan's Perak enterprise, the Siamese ordered Sultan Ahmad Taju'd-din to send one hundred war-boats, and rice, to assist Thai forces resist a Burmese invasion of Thailand which never materialized. The Siamese further forbade the Kedah sultan to export rice to Penang, hoping thereby to embitter his relations with the British.[14] The Thai-Kedah dialogue was finally attended with war in 1821 when Sultan Ahmad Taju'd-din refused to attend a summons to appear at Bangkok to answer charges leveled against his loyalty to King Rama II. In a brief campaign Thai forces, commanded by the governor of Ligor, cruelly devastated the sultanate of Kedah and forced Sultan Ahmad Taju'd-din to flee to British territory and Company protection.[15]

EXTRACT OF THE LETTER FROM THE GOVERNOR OF PENANG TO THE GOVERNOR GENERAL OF INDIA, LORD HASTINGS, FORT WILLIAM AT CALCUTTA

Dated, 28th November 1821

"Having succeeded in capturing the chief town, and the person of the principal Minister, and putting to death several other persons of rank, the [Siamese] enemy proceeded to Pulo Tega in the Murbow, up which river the Rajah had fixed his residence, from which after a trifling resistance His Highness was obliged to fly into the Company's territories, leaving behind him the greater part of his Treasure, and losing the remainder, and several of his Adherents in his journey through the forests." [16]

The governor of Ligor demanded the surrender of the sultan, but was rebuffed by Governor Phillips of Penang. The Siamese had sufficient sense not to test conclusions by arms with the powerful British East India Company, no longer the mere humble trading concern of former years, but the paramount power of India with the resources of Hindustan at its beck and call. Company soldiers were dispatched to Province Wellesley to prevent Thai pursuit of Kedah fugitives on British soil. Tension mounted as trade relations between the mainland and Penang were disrupted and Province Wellesley threatened with possible Siamese attack.[17]

The period of rising tension, and conflict of interest, between the Kingdom of Siam and the East India Company coincided with a renewal of British commercial interest in Siam, long dormant following the closure of the English factory in 1684. In 1821 the British settlement of Singapore, established in 1819, dispatched the merchant John Morgan to establish direct commercial contact with the Kingdom of Siam. Morgan sailed from Singapore on April 25, 1821 in a small boat of seventy tons, the *Non me recordo*, with a letter from the resident councillor of Singapore, Colonel Farquhar, addressed to the king of Siam. Mr. Morgan arrived in Thailand in May, and on June 5th, 1821 John Morgan, British merchant, was granted an audience with Rama II, king of Siam, and the letter to the king was read aloud.[18]

LETTER FROM THE RESIDENT COUNCILLOR OF SINGAPORE TO THE KING OF SIAM

After Compliments

"I beg to acquaint Your Majesty that about two years back the English formed a Settlement in the Straits of Singapore, from which period till the present, no vessel actually belonging to the port has cleared out for Siam, but as there is now a small schooner, the property of English merchants here, about to proceed thither, I cannot permit so favourable an opportunity to pass without addressing Your Majesty the present letter, for the purpose of informing Your Majesty of the new Establishment the British Government has formed here, trusting that it may be the means of strengthening the ties of friendship and reciprocity of kindness between Siam and Singapore in all commercial affairs. Every description of Siamese goods find a ready sale here, particularly such as are at present imported by the Chinese junks sailing out of Your Majesty's ports, and numerous articles in demand at Siam are procurable here.

"I send this letter by Mr. John Morgan, a respectable English merchant residing here, whom I beg leave to recommend to your Majesty's favour and protection. Mr. Morgan will be able to afford such further information respecting this settlement as Your Majesty may require.

"I regret that I have nothing of suitable value to send your Majesty but as a token of friendship and respect beg Your Majesty's acceptance of a Double Barrel Gun and two mirrors." [19]

(Signed) W. FARQUHAR
Singapore
9th April, 1821.

John Morgan was permitted to engage in trade but without success. His furtive commerce in opium, contrary to Siamese law, was not unperceived by the authorities and as unlikely to allay Thai suspicion as advance moral rectitude. The East India Company, we conclude, had not yet discovered the elixir to improved Anglo-Siamese relations notwithstanding the accumulated experience of previous intercourse and sustained effort. Morgan concluded his mission at a financial loss, departed Siam with nine pieces of ivory and a quantity of sugar, presents from King Rama II. Morgan billed the Penang government for $5,200 as recompense for losses previously guaranteed, and the Calcutta government which footed the bill paid Morgan $1,200 for personal expenses and his company $3,612 for their losses. Morgan's mission reports were received by John Crawfurd.[20]

In September 1821 the governor-general of India, the marquis of Hastings, deputed John Crawfurd of the Medical Service on a mission to the courts of Siam and Cochin China (or Vietnam).[21] Crawfurd was instructed by the governor-general to seek removal of restrictions, which obstructed British and British-Indian commerce with Siam and Vietnam, and the improvement of Anglo-Thai relations on the subject of Kedah.[22]

EXTRACT OF THE LETTER OF INSTRUCTIONS FROM THE GOVERNOR-GENERAL OF INDIA TO JOHN CRAWFURD CONCERNING HIS MISSION TO SIAM AND VIETNAM

Dated, 29th September 1821

"You are aware, that in the earlier period of the Indian commerce of the European nations, the trade of Siam and Cochin China constituted no unimportant branch of it; and that during their struggle for superiority among themselves in India, and those contests with the native powers which led to the establishment of territorial possessions, the commerce with those two countries was overlooked or neglected; so that, during the first half of the last century, that trade became extremely inconsiderable, and during the last seventy years may be looked upon as having altogether ceased.

"From the most authentic information in the possession of this Government, there is every reason to believe that the industry and civilization, together with the geographical position and natural fertility of soil which characterise the kingdoms of Siam and Cochin China, are such as to render it extremely desirable, under the present stagnation of trade, to negotiate with the Sovereigns of those countries the renewal of a commercial intercourse with Great Britain and her Indian dominions . . . [and] . . . Although the Governor-General in

Council is solicitous to avoid mixing any thing of a political nature with your negotiations at Siam, it seems desirable that you should be in possession of the grounds on which the Governor of Penang has felt an anxiety for the security of the States of Queda and Pera [Perak]; and that you should be prepared to avail yourself of any favourable opportunity of accomplishing the wishes of the Governor [of Penang] in Council [in furtherance of British Malayan interests] by a friendly and unostentatious representation to the Court of Siam." [23]

John Crawfurd, envoy extraordinary, embarked from Calcutta, India, on November 21st, 1821 for the voyage to Siam as well as Vietnam.[24] Arriving at Bangkok on March 29, 1822,[25] after a leisurely voyage, Crawfurd presented a letter from the governor-general of India to the appropriate Siamese official for translation and presentation to King Rama II.[26]

EXTRACT OF THE LETTER FROM THE GOVERNOR-GENERAL OF INDIA TO THE KING OF SIAM

"In token of the esteem and respect of the English nation for your Majesty, I send into your presence my Envoy . . . [with earnest desire for friendship and intercourse between the British and Siamese nations &&&] . . .

"I desire from your Majesty neither port, settlement, fort, nor factories; neither do I claim that our merchants resorting to your Majesty's country should be exempted from the authority of its laws. But if any regulation of your Majesty's Government touching foreign commerce should be found to bear hard upon our merchants, and thereby prove an obstacle to the extension of their trade with your Majesty's dominions, I shall trust to your Majesty's wisdom and friendly disposition to have them modified or removed." [27]

John Crawfurd was greeted by the P'rak'lang on the evening of March 29th, and the latter promised the British envoy an early audience with the king of Siam.[28] No particular difficulty was encountered arranging the mode of obeisance, requested of the foreigner in the royal presence. The act of prostration was waived, and Crawfurd with retinue, when in the presence of King Rama II, was requested to bow in the European fashion, be seated and make obeisance to the Siamese king by raising joined hands to the forehead.[29] On April 8, 1822 four (or five) members of the British mission headed by John Crawfurd were conducted to the audience hall of the Royal Palace at Bangkok.

"Opposite to the door of the hall of audience there was an immense Chinese mirror, of many parts, which formed a screen, concealing the interior of the Court from our view. We had no sooner arrived at this spot than a loud flourish of wind instruments was heard, accompanied by a wild shout or yell, which announced, as we afterwards found, the arrival of his Majesty. We passed the screen to the right side, and, as had been agreed upon, taking off our hats, made a respectful bow in the European manner. Every foot of the great hall

131

which we had now entered was literally so crowded with prostrate courtiers, that it was difficult to move without the risk
of treading upon some officer of state. Precedence is decided,
upon such occasions, by relative vicinity to the throne; the
princes being near the foot of it, the principal officers of Government next to them, and thus in succession down to the
lowest officer who is admitted into the presence. We seated
ourselves a little in front of the screen, and made three obei-
sances to the throne, in unison with the courtiers. This
obeisance consisted in raising the joined hands to the head
three times, and at each touching the forehead." [30]

King Rama II inquired the nature of the mission, the health of the governor-
general of India and other miscellanies through an interpreter. Receiving suitable replies to his different questions, King Rama II concluded the interview on
the following note:

'"I am glad to see an envoy here from the Governor-general
of India. Whatever you have to say, communicate to the
minister, Suri-wung-kosa [the P'rak'lang]. What we chiefly
want from you are fire-arms."' [31]

Thereupon curtains to the right and left of the throne closed upon the regal
setting, concealing the king of Siam from the humble British petitioners. [32]

Before continuing with the results of the British embassy to the court of
Siam, I solicit the attention of the reader for a discussion of life in Old Siam in
the days before the collapse of the ancient state under the vigorous assault of
western influences during the nineteenth century. John Crawfurd, in the *Journal
of an Embassy from the Governor-General of India to the Courts of Siam and
Cochin China* and in a report of his mission to Siam directed to the Indian government, has preserved for posterity a vivid and factual account of his impres-
sions of the Thai people and state, as it existed during the second decade of
the nineteenth century.

Crawfurd, for instance, estimates the population of Siam at about five
million persons including four million and two hundred thousand of the Thai
race and seven hundred thousand of Chinese extraction. The Chinese were scattered throughout the country chiefly at the centers of commerce. The Chinese at
Bangkok constituted about one-half of the population. [33]

Nature blessed the bountiful soil of Thailand with mineral, forest, agricul-
tural and animal wealth. Mineral produce included iron mined north of the
capital. The Chinese apparently dominated the smelting and manufacture of
iron in Siam. Iron was exported to Cambodia, Cochin China and the islands of
the Indian Archipelago forming a valuable export commodity. Iron in Siam
was wrought into culinary utensils and other implements. Tin was mined, exclu-
sively by the Siamese, and also exported.

Valuable products of Thai forests include teakwood, little of which was
exported, rosewood exported to China in large quantities and sappanwood also
an important export commodity in the Siamese economy. In addition a precious
perfume called agila or eagle was a valuable article of commerce in the markets
of western Asia. [34]

Among the staple products of Thai agriculture Crawfurd lists rice, sugar,
pepper and tobacco.

"The great rice country is of course the tract subjected to the inundations of the Me-nam. This portion of the country is of remarkable fertility and yields rice with a comparatively small portion of labour, so that there is no place where in ordinary years grain can be had at a cheaper rate than in Siam.[35]

Sugar cane was grown on the island of Junk Ceylon and probably elsewhere in Siam at least as early as the eighteenth century and perhaps earlier,[36] although Crawfurd erroneously ascribes the introduction of sugar cane in Siam to a Chinese agency about the year 1810. Pepper was successfully cultured by the Chinese on the east coast of the Gulf of Siam and exported to China in large quantities. The king of Siam maintained a partial monopoly of the pepper trade, and the Kingdom of Siam competed with the island of Sumatra as a world center of pepper production. Before the year 1800 tobacco was largely imported from Sumatra, but by the year of Crawfurd's visit (1822) the Siamese were exporting large quantities of tobacco to Cambodia and Cochin China.

Animal produce of the kingdom, including the skins of deer, buffalo, the elephant, rhinoceros, tiger, leopard, otter and the cat; rhinoceros horns, ivory, feathers and salt fish, were important articles of export the commerce of which was dominated by the Chinese.[37]

The Siamese imports largely consisted of the manufactures of China including manufactured silk, common earthenware, porcelain, paper, toys, wearing apparel and also tea. From India the Thais received opium and cotton piece goods. Products from India were shipped from Batavia and the Malacca Straits by junk or direct from India by European shipping. Among European manufactures cotton goods, cheap woolens, glassware and firearms were in demand.

Crawfurd estimates the amount and value of the Siamese foreign trade as second only to China among east Asian states. Bangkok was the emporium of Thai commerce, and the funnel through which commerce of Siam was channeled to and from China. The foreign trade of the Thai kingdom was dominated by the Chinese, resident in Siam and the Chinese Empire. The Chinese, in the first quarter of the nineteenth century, commanded and navigated the shipping of Siam engaged in the China trade, including ships owned by Chinese merchants or those owned by the king of Siam, the princes and members of the court. However, many (if not most) of the vessels employed in the China trade were constructed in Siam.

John Crawfurd furnishes, in terms of shipping, the following breakdown of the annual Siamese export trade at the time of his visit to Siam:

To the Port of Canton	8 Junks
To the Ports of the Island of Hainan	40 Small Junks
To the Ports of Fukien, Chekiang and Kiangnan	32 Junks
To Batavia	3 Junks
To Singapore	27 Small Junks
To Malacca and Penang	5 Junks
To China from Ligor	2 Junks
To China from Chantibun (Chanthaburi)	1 Junk
To Saigon	18 Small Junks
Total	136 Junks

The Siamese could expect visits from a few British, American and Malay ships as well as perhaps an infrequent Portuguese or Dutch merchantman willing to gather the produce of the land in exchange for various sundries, albeit with a current of Thai suspicion which ran against western vessels attending their ascent of the Menam River.[38]

The revenue of the Thai kingdom was derived from a number of sources including a land tax levied in kind on rice, a money tax levied on certain fruit trees as well as a money tax on tobacco and sugar cane. A tax was imposed by the government on selected fisheries, a duty on shops rated according to the nature of the trade, and we might add a tax on gambling—an important source of royal revenue but a vice to which the Siamese were particularly addicted. Other sources of royal income included a capitation tax on the Chinese population, frequently evaded, custom duties and a duty upon the tonnage or measurement of merchant vessels. Chinese merchants received preferential treatment. The Chinese junks trading with mainland China were not subject to impost on goods (imported or exported) or duties on tonnage. Ships belonging to merchants of the ports of Hainan, however, were obliged to pay a measurement duty.

But the chief source of governmental revenue derived from the royal monopoly which the king of Siam exercised over select articles of Siamese commerce. King Rama II obliged both his Thai subjects and the resident Chinese to sell the monopoly product for a consideration less than its market value. Marketing on the principle of buying cheap and selling dear, the king could expect to reap a handsome profit. The royal monopoly, however, to the credit of the throne, did not extend to those articles which might be deemed necessaries of life, but encompassed such diverse objects as the commerce of cardamons, gamboge, sappanwood, eaglewood, benjamin, ivory, tin, esculent nests and turtle eggs.[39] The royal government also maintained a partial monopoly of the pepper and sugar trades.[40] Crawfurd estimates the revenue and expenditure of the central government were nearly balanced, or about two to three million ticals in money annually.* [41]

A heavy imposition placed upon the people of Thailand was exacted by the government neither in taxes of money or kind, but in labor or corvee service demanded of commoners from three to four (or more) months each year.

> "The way in which this obligation was controlled represented a curious survival from feudal times. Every free man was responsible to a patron, who originally had been a feudal lord but by Bangkok times had become a government official. The type of work done by a free man, civil or military, depended on the department of the patron. To keep manpower requirements stable, the government discouraged the people from exercising their traditional right to change patrons. . . . During his period of service, which was usually distributed through the year in one-month periods, the free man received no reimbursement of any kind; no food or lodging was provided. In addition to the ordinary requirement of three months, additional labor could be required at any time for special undertakings."[42]

---

* One tical was worth perhaps sixty cents during the early 1800s.

When burdened by debt, the Thai freeman could sell himself and family into slavery. The patron would therefore lose his services and hence, if only for reasons of self-interest, the patron sought to avert, among his dependents, situations of desperate financial impairment. Moreover corvee service was usually commutable by a money payment.

Slavery was widespread in Siamese society during the early nineteenth century, and perhaps one-third of the population of the kingdom labored in servitude to a master rather than a patron. The master, after delivery of prescribed royal dues, maintained exclusive right to the service of his human chattel. In certain instances the status of debt and pagoda slaves approached that of the Thai freeman.[43]

Crawfurd is unstinting in his denunciation of the rapacity, vanity, indolence and despotism of the government of Siam. Corruption flourished at virtually all levels of administration, and the courtiers servile toward their superiors were domineering toward the lower orders of Thai society. Crawfurd asserts the population of Bangkok partook of the vices of their leaders, although he assures us the character of the Thais in the provinces was more favorable. Nevertheless hostile as Crawfurd viewed many aspects of the Thai state and people he was not, for that reason, unwilling to recognize their virtues. He describes the Thai as a law-abiding people, distinguished from the Malays by their lack of a spirit of revenge. Parental affection was strong. Thai women were temperate and not veiled, or secluded, as in many Asian countries. They were generally well treated, but viewed as lesser creatures than members of the opposite sex. The enforced conscription of the men for government service threw an extra work load on the female population, who were obliged to perform excessive manual labor. The rich, including King Rama II who maintained three hundred wives, practiced polygamy, but the lower orders were monogamous.[44]

John Crawfurd engaged the P'rak'lang in a number of conferences, but was unable to persuade the Siamese to reduce the import duty on goods in British ships or to allow British merchants freedom of disposal of lawful merchandise. The P'rak'lang, for his part, wished to know if the Indian government would deliver the sultan of Kedah to the Siamese if so requested by King Rama II. Crawfurd assured the P'rak'lang that the supreme government of India would not deliver the sultan for Thai disposition. Suspicion and distrust remained strong on both sides.[45] However, the Thai government, by silence on the subject of the British occupation of Penang and Province Wellesley, recognized the de facto British title to territories which the Siamese once claimed in suzerainty. The Siamese, cognizant of an inability to enforce a claim, were too prudent to assert by force of arms what they would not attempt by diplomacy.[46]

Crawfurd terminated his embassy to Siam without assurances that British merchants would be free to dispose of lawful merchandise; nor did he acquire for his countrymen a reduction of the rate of impost placed upon British commerce with the Kingdom of Siam. He did, however, receive an assurance that the duties would not be raised against British trade in the future.[47] Crawfurd, however, was convinced the British had little to fear from the Siamese militarily, and that Penang was safe from attack.[48] Crawfurd departed Siam in mid-1822 for Vietnam and the continuation of his embassy as enjoined in his instructions from the governor-general of India.

King Rama II lived for two years following the close of the Crawfurd embassy to Siam. He died on July 21st, 1824, at the age of fifty-six.*[49] Rama II was a man of artistic inclination, composing poetry and sculpturing as well. During his reign the tower of the Wat Arun was partially constructed (and completed in the following reign).[50] The reign of King Rama II is especially noteworthy for the final expulsion of the Burmese, the aggrandizement of the Thai Kingdom on the Cambodian frontier, and the faint renewal of western contacts (so pregnant in meaning for the future of the Thai people).

---

* King Rama II became faint, followed by stiffness in the joints, and then lapsed into a coma before death.

BIBLIOGRAPHY

1. *Arquivos de Macau*, Vol. I, No. 2, 1929.
2. Cady, John F. *Southeast Asia—Its Historical Development*, McGraw-Hill Book Company, 1964.
3. Chula, H.R.H. Prince. *Lords of Life*, Taplinger Publishing Co., Inc., New York, 1960.
4. Cowan, C. D. "Early Penang & the Rise of Singapore 1805-1832," *Journal of the Malayan Branch of the Royal Asiatic Society*, Vol. XXIII, Part 2, Singapore, 1950.
5. Crawfurd, John. *Journal of an Embassy from the Governor-General of India to the Courts of Siam and Cochin China*, London, 1828.
6. *Crawfurd Papers, The.* Printed by order of the Vajiranana National Library, Bangkok, 1915.
7. Frankfurter, O. "The Unofficial Mission of John Morgan, merchant, to Siam in 1821," *Journal of the Siam Society*, Vol. XI, Part 1, Bangkok, 1914.
8. Gerini, G. E. "Historical Retrospect of Junkceylon Island," *Journal of the Siam Society*, Vol. II, Part 2, Bangkok, 1905.
9. Kennedy, J. *A History of Malaya* A.D. 1400-1959, St. Martin's Press, 1962.
10. Maybon, Charles B. *Histoire Moderne du Pays D'Annam (1592-1820)*, Typographie Plon-Nourrit et Cie, Paris, 1919.
11. Moura, J. *Le Royaume du Cambodge*, Vol. II, Paris, 1883.
12. *Scattergoods and the East India Company, The.* The British India Press, Bombay, 1921-33, and D. J. Jeffrey Ltd., Harpenden, 1935. Being a selection of the papers of John Scattergood, East India merchant, 1681-1723.
13. Vella, Walter F. *Siam under Rama III*, J. J. Augustin Incorporated Publisher, Locust Valley, N.Y., 1957.
14. Winstedt, Sir Richard O. "A History of Perak," *Journal of the Malayan Branch of the Royal Asiatic Society*, Vol. XII, Part 1, Singapore, 1934.

FOOTNOTES

1. Prince Chula, 117.
2. Gerini, 72-82.
3. Maybon, 382.
4. Moura, 105.

5. Arquivos de Macau, 95, 96.
6. Frankfurter, 6.
7. Crawfurd, 104, 105.
8. The Crawfurd Papers, 160, 161.
9. Ibid., 119.
10. Ibid., 161, 162.
11. Crawfurd, 158, 159.
12. The Crawfurd Papers, 161.
13. Winstedt, 64-66.
14. Ibid., 65.
15. Kennedy, 106.
16. Cowan, 122.
17. Kennedy, 107.
18. Frankfurter, 3, 4.
19. Ibid., 8.
20. Ibid., 3-7.
21. Crawfurd, 1.
22. Ibid., 589-95.
23. Crawfurd, 589, 593, 594.
24. Ibid., 2.
25. Ibid., 78.
26. Ibid., 80, 81.
27. Ibid., 595, 596.
28. Ibid., 81, 82.
29. Ibid., 88.
30. Ibid., 92, 93.
31. Ibid., 94, 95.
32. Ibid., 95.
33. The Crawfurd Papers, 102-04.
34. Ibid., 108-10.
35. Ibid., 111.
36. The Scattergoods, etc., 104.
37. The Crawfurd Papers, 111-13.
38. Ibid., 114-21.
39. Ibid., 129-33.
40. Crawfurd, 380.
41. Ibid., 388, 389.
42. Vella, 20, 21.
43. Cady, 328.
44. Crawfurd, 342-49.
45. Ibid., 163-65.
46. Ibid., 160.
47. Ibid., 172-74.
48. Cady, 333.
49. Prince Chula, 142.
50. Ibid., 138-40.

APPENDIX I

The Burmese Siege of Ayudhya (1587) and the Subsequent Invasion of Cambodia by King Naresuen as described in the *Luang Prasoet* Chronicle of Siamese History.

In 948, the year of the dog, on Monday the 8th of the 12th waning moon, the King of Pegu Ngachisayang [Nanda Bayin] proceeded to the capital. On Thursday the 2nd of the 2nd waxing moon he arrived before the capital and established his camp at Khanon Pak Khu. The army of the Mahauparaj was established at Khanon Bang Tanao, and the enemy made preparations for surrounding the capital, and at that time constant fighting was going on. The King, on Monday the 14th of the 5th waxing moon 947 [948?], raised his army and proceeded by boat to attack the army of the Mahauparaj established at Khanon Bang Tanao. It retired to Bang Kradan on Friday the 10th of the 6th waning moon, the King defeated the army of the Mahauparaj at Bang Kradan again and it was scattered. On Thursday the 1st of the 7th waxing moon the King established his camp at Wat Dej, and entrenched it. On Thursday the 8th of the 7th waxing moon he put guns on the junks and bombarded the camp of the King of Pegu, who could not resist and retired to Pa-mok Yai. On Monday the 10th of the 4th waxing moon the King attacked the enemies, who were then defeated, and he drove them back, armed with a sword, towards camp. On Tuesday the 10th of the 4th waning moon the King established his camp in an ambush at Lomphli, and entered into a battle with the enemy. The battle was carried on with great courage, the King fought on horseback, and many soldiers were killed by his own sword. The soldiers were defeated and returned to camp, to which they were pursued.

On Monday the 10th of the third waning moon, at 7 a.m., the King attacked the army of Phraya Nakhon, which was established at Paknam Muthulao. At that time he attacked the camp from which the enemy fled after a great loss. The king of Pegu then disbanded his army and retired, when Phraya Lavek [the king of Cambodia] established himself at Bang Sai. At that time the King collected his whole army at Bang Kradan, and on Thursday the 1st of the 3rd waxing moon, at the auspicious moment, he proceeded from Bang Kradan and established his headquarters at Sai Khuang, and from there he proceeded to Lavek [Cambodia]. At that time the King captured many elephants and horses, and many people were made prisoners.

APPENDIX II

The first Spanish Embassy dispatched to the Kingdom of Siam as related by Don Francisco Tello, the Governor of the Philippines, to Philip III, the King of Spain, in his Official Letter:

Dated, 12th July 1599 (N.S.)

After I came to this government, I received the letter of the King of Siam, of which a copy will be made, of those things which he said to me, namely that he had desire for communication and dealing with these isles of Your Majesty and for my part seeing such a good will in this King, I dispatched the Captain Joan Tello [de Aguirre] in the past year of 1598 with an embassy for the King in reply, the purport of it being that he values the friendship which he offers and desire which he has for the dealings with the Spanish in his Kingdom, offering in the name of Your Majesty all correspondence. The Captain Joan Tello made the voyage and . . . also the transactions, the result of it being that he allowed open ports and trading so that the Spanish will be induced to come and test it, free and free of duties, and he returned with the answer of the King of Siam bringing in his ship some benjamin, ivory and stones for the residents of this city . . .

APPENDIX III

11th August 1664 (O.S.)
22nd August 1664 (N.S.)

Agreement and closer Alliance of Peace made and concluded between his Majesty the King of Siam on the one side and Commissary Pieter de Bitter on the other, deputy of the Governor General Jan Maetsuijcker and Council of India ruling (in the name and on the behalf of the high and mighty States General of the United Netherlands) the State of the United East India Company in the East.

Firstly, it is agreed, concluded and determined, that from now onwards and henceforth a just, inviolable, secure, sincere alliance and friendship shall exist and be maintained between the King of Siam and the Netherlands Company, together with the subjects of both, and that from this day onwards such questions, differences and further disputes as have arisen between his Majesty's subjects and the Company shall be put out of mind and never more thought of, provided the King punishes and shall punish duly and as they deserve the authors of the affronts done to the Company.

Secondly, it is agreed that henceforth the Company shall enjoy in Siam, Ligor, Oetjangh, Salangh, and all other places and lands of the King, without exception, the peaceful, undisturbed exercise of trade in all such goods and merchandize as are to be found in each [place], without reservation of any nature whatever.

Item. That the Company shall have power to trade, deal and correspond with all and any persons that they choose, be they of high or low degree, without let or hindrance, either direct or indirect, from any person whatsoever.

Further it is agreed and determined, that neither now nor hereafter shall the Company be charged with nor have raised against them in any manner whatever, higher duties etc. on imported or exported goods and merchandize, be it in Siam, Ligor, Oetjangh, Salangh or anywhere else, but shall satisfy and pay all dues according to former custom, as has been stipulated and agreed in the statutory ordinance of the King.

Item. It is agreed that neither now nor hereafter shall his Majesty the King or his subjects, of whatsoever station they may be, have the power to place any Chinese, viz., the inhabitants of Japan, Canton, Cochin-China, Tonquin, on their junks, ships or smaller vessels, much less to endeavour to introduce men of that nation within their boundaries; that all junks and ships on which natives of that country shall be found, if met by ours at sea, shall be seized as prizes and the Company shall not be bound at any time to make any restitution.

139

Further, it is agreed and determined that the said Company shall for all time have the exportation of all the deerskins and cowhides which come to Siam, as also the retailing of all other merchandize from any other nation or of any kind, and his Majesty shall be bound by all means to maintain the Company in this privilege.

Moreover, if it should happen that any debtors refuse to make their payments to the Company, as has formerly happened frequently, his Majesty shall, through Oja Berckelangh, the advocate of the foreigners, give his assistance, and those debtors he shall keep in strict confinement until the Company shall have received its own, and in case the Company shall fail to secure payment of just claims by these means, then the King or Oja Berckelang shall be bound to hand over said debtors to the Company.

In case (which God forbid) any of the Company's residents should commit a serious crime in Siam, the King and the judges shall not have the right to judge him, but he must be handed over to the Company's chief to be punished according to the Netherlands laws, and if it shall happen that the said Chief was his accomplice in a capital offence, his Majesty is to have the power to keep them both confined in their own houses until he has sent word of the matter to the Governor General. . . .

APPENDIX IV

Text of the Letter of Constantine Phaulkon to Father Tachard, Dated October 3rd, 1687, at the Time of the Arrival (at the Bar of Siam) of the French Expedition commanded by Marshal Desfarges. Father Tachard was charged with making the necessary arrangements for the disembarkation of the French troops.

My Reverend Father

I have duly considered what Your Reverence represents to me regarding the Royal Wishes of His Most Christian Majesty [i.e. King Louis XIV of France], truly worthy of his Greatness and Glory. For my part, besides the obligations I owe His Majesty because of his royal favors and honors, the ones I owe Our Lord for His infinite mercy and compassion are so obvious to the world that I do not need to reaffirm them except in the form of gratitude that my designs for the propagation of the Roman Catholic Faith, and its defense in this Kingdom are in accord with the wishes of His Most Christian Majesty, without whose patronage and royal hand, this would be impossible, because I am truly convinced that Our Lord has made this choice of His Most Christian Majesty, as the first-born of His Holy Church, to assume such a great task on which depends and in which rests the great possibility of the entire conversion of the Orient, that it does not need more urging. Taking this into consideration, and assuming that he is His instrument, Your Reverence may well judge the favorable path these matters are following. But, as the service of Our Lord in this world conforms to a great extent to justice, righteousness and truth, it is advisable to reflect on what a change of government in France—which God, through His infinite mercy may expand—could produce in the speech of the world, which does not know my intentions and, particularly, in the speech of the wicked.

Your Reverence represents to me that the wishes of His Majesty consist of three points: first, the protection of the [Christian] Religion; second, the service

140

of His Majesty, the King of Siam; and third, commercial matters, about which Your Reverency offers an explanation.

For the security of Religion, he [the king] said, it would be necessary to fortify a very important place in the Kingdom of Siam so that, in case of a change in the government, Christianity would not be exposed to the insults of malevolents, and be totally destroyed, and as no other place seems more convenient to His Most Christian Majesty than the city of Bangkok he requests, therefore, His Majesty of Siam to entrust the guard of this stronghold to the officers and soldiers that His Most Christian Majesty sends for this end, and to permit him to fortify it after the European manner for the service of the abovementioned King of Siam; and that His Most Christian Majesty sends, for this purpose, troops, officers, engineers, etc. to render their services to the abovementioned King of Siam in any manner he may see fit.

Regarding commerce which is of interest to both of the parties, His Most Christian Majesty would be most pleased if His Majesty the King of Siam, his good friend, would grant him the means to assure the French of their trade in case of war with Holland because the Dutch are Lords of all the ways leading to the Kingdom of Siam and he does not doubt that His Majesty, due to the deep bonds of friendship between the two Crowns, will arrange matters in such a manner that the subjects of France will remain secure in their possessions, and that His Most Christian Majesty, by the advice which he has, believes that the Port of Merguy should be governed in the same manner as Bangkok [that is in the power of the French], then this issue will be well provided.

In these explanations of Your Reverence I observe three points:

1st—The great piety of His Most Christian Majesty for the propagation of the Catholic Faith to which end (notwithstanding all the inconveniences of the great distances and the dangers represented) His Most Christian Majesty (so great is his royal spirit and zeal for God's service) has exposed his vassals and royal treasures as succor for anything which may happen, and meanwhile obligating His Majesty, my Master, with favors worthy of such a monarch, while at the same time preserving a place of great importance in this Kingdom for its service and its defense—offering his vassals for any service His Majesty, my Master, may wish.

2nd—That His Majesty considering how inconvenient it is to expose French troops at fortified places, according to the manner of the Orient, and guided by his royal amity and [wish for the] preservation of the Kingdom of his friend, my Master, he [Louis XIV] resolved to send, at his expense, engineers to work toward this end.

3rd—As the Dominions of His Majesty, my Master, are so vast, with so many ingresses, preserving one without the other can be the cause of great inconveniences and unrest, threatening the peace and tranquility of these Dominions, as well as the reciprocal assistance of troops without which they would be left unprotected, His Most Christian Majesty appointed the Port of Merguy as the second [port], as the more important one on that side, and with this he surely guarantees the commerce so reciprocally beneficial to both of the two crowns.

And so His Most Christian Majesty ensures the propagation of the Faith, and provisionally succors His Majesty, my Lord, with art, experience and power for any situation which may arise. Any person truly devoted to the honor of

His Majesty, my Lord, and to the preservation of the important fortified places, will judge that these were the true and sole motives which led His Most Christian Majesty to take the present course of action. However, Your Reverence well knows the wicked times in which we live, and how people are apt to make mountains out of nothing and nothing into mountains; and, confirming their suppositions with the circumstances which at the present juncture in time permit the bestowal of honors and favors by His Most Christian Majesty (which he has been pleased to make) divers persons might be convinced that I was led to the infamy of becoming disloyal to the King, my Lord, by advising him to entrust his fortified places to alien powers, without occasion, a thing which I would never do, even if I were to gain the world. Since Your Reverence knows that it was God's will to lead me along a path that since the beginning of my life was filled with diverse manner of occurrences, and which led me to the position I am now holding; so that I, seeing the diverse vanities of this world, I would disregard all except that which alone pertains to God's Glory (which very much agrees with the wishes of His Most Christian Majesty), for he seeks more than just the sole administration of so many states which are subject to the King, my Lord, and the appointment of persons to office in these states, and [I] rejoice in a closer grace and favor of such a well-meaning gentleman; it is certainly true (my Father) that even my own father would not treat me with such benevolence. Assuming this, I feel that I can be sure that no man of address and consideration could slander me; but, on the other hand, I am sure that the opposite is true among the malevolents and, as Your Reverence well knows, there are some French among them; but I have always taken these things into consideration—[consideration being] the only weapon I have used against them—and, therefore, there are no reasons to prevent me to effect negotiations directed toward the service of Our Lord God, from whom His Majesty, my Master, and his successors may attain much felicity and the commonalty much peace and rest in this life and glory in the next.

Your Reverence has stated that the envoys extraordinary sent by His Most Christian Majesty came to discuss these things with me, and with view to security before disembarkation, he gave them instructions which, because of the trust Your Reverence places in me, you offered to show me.

My Reverend Father, the instructions have two qualities: first, power; and second, directions; both provisional. Regarding the first one, I assume correctly . . . that Your Reverence will come to discuss with me the letter of M. de Seignelay, representing the King, his Master, dated in Versailles on January 22nd, 1687, the honor being sufficient for me to have an emissary deal and come to the final conclusions with me.

And about the directions, I shall include them so I will not be lengthy. The reason for the directions was concern for safety before disembarking, which infers, I am sorry to say, that Their Excellencies have little confidence in us—which does not accord with the favors of His Majesty, under whose royal hand they were given, but they were guided by the ways of true politics and not by friendship and confidence. We could reciprocate with the same policy; but taking into consideration the great obligations I have towards Our Lord God, to whose service these things are dedicated, and the respect I feel for the guidance from His Most Christian Majesty, granting that His Most Christian Majesty and his successors will attest to our fidelity and loyalty which we owe first to God, and to His Majesty the King of Siam, my Master and great benefactor; we, by this, promise that His Majesty, my Master, may grant, as soon as possible, all that Your Reverence has proposed. But I may caution Your Reverence to tell Their Excellencies that, as concerns His Most Christian Majesty, to order the officers in charge of the boats and of the troops that, when disembarking at Bangkok to refresh and to cure their sick, even though they are in charge of the garrison, to behave at all times with circumspection, so that no one may have cause for complaint, especially regarding these [before-mentioned] principles, and that Their Excellencies make an instrument of particular articles: that these troops must follow our orders, and that, for the security [of the realm] no one besides His Majesty the King of Siam and I, shall assume the command (which will be the condition in the oath which they will render to His Siamese Majesty) so we may examine and conclude this matter, in order that these troops may take over speedily. And so I shall finish this present letter, signed in our house, on October third, of the year one thousand six hundred and eighty-seven.

Your very humble servant and good brother

Counselor Phaulkon

KINGS OF THE THAIS

AYUDHYA

T'ONBURI

BANGKOK PERIOD

Having fathomed the secrets of the African seas, rounded the Cape of Storms, and burst upon the unknown wastes of the Indian Ocean; the Portuguese nation toppled the sultan of Malacca from his entrepotal throne, overturned his kingdom in 1511, and then marched in triumph to the reaches of furthest Asia. Treading roads untouched by Christian feet, the same bold nation directed her steps to the Kingdom of Siam, not in war, but in peace and friendship.

The Kingdoms of Siam and Portugal, situated at the extremities of the earth, and separated by a wide chasm of religious, political and cultural divergence, were nevertheless joined in amity as the result of three embassies dispatched from Malacca to the court of Ayudhya.

Of the original Portuguese sources relating to the first embassies to the Kingdom of Siam, few are extant, and those remaining are comprehended in the works of four eminent Portuguese historians of the sixteenth century: Damião de Goes, João de Barros, Fernão Lopez de Castanheda and Gaspar Correa. Extracts from the histories of de Goes and de Barros are translated below as they relate to the embassies of Duarte Fernandez in 1511 (and his return with a Siamese ambassador in the same year), Miranda de Azevedo in 1512 and Duarte Coelho. The great British historian of the Thai people, W. A. R. Wood, assigns the date of Coelho's embassy to the year 1516, but João de Barros ascribes his embassy to the period 1518-19.

THE EMBASSY OF DUARTE FERNANDEZ (1511) TO THE KING OF SIAM AND HIS RETURN WITH THE AMBASSADOR OF THE KING OF SIAM AS DESCRIBED BY DAMIAM DE GOES (1502-1574)

Since the season for navigation was passing, the captains of the junks from China asked licence of Affonso de Albuquerque [to depart], which he gave to them as well as provisions which they had not been able to procure from the city, and because one of them called Pulata had to go to the city of Siam, he requested that he take with him a Portuguese from those who were captives with Ruy de Araujo, by the name of Duarte Fernandez, who knew the Malayan language, commanding him to visit the King of Siam, giving to him account of what he had done at Malacca, offering it to him, since in the said city (which he expects in God to gain very soon) he desires to gather all the Siamese who wish to live there, by which messenger he sent to him an adorned sword of enamelled gold with his sword belt of the same trappings . . .

Duarte Fernandez, whom Affonso de Albuquerque had sent to the King of Siam, returned after giving his embassy in the city of Ayudhya, and with him came an ambassador from the King, who wrote to him as to whatever he might accomplish in his kingdom, that he should judge of it very completely, and to him he sent a ring with a very rich ruby, and a long golden rapier, a goblet of gold, with a letter for the King Dom Manuel, in which he wrote that he was well pleased to see him lord of Malacca and to have for his neighbors his captains to whom he would grant all necessary favors. By the same ambassador he sent to the hand of the Viceroy Affonso de Albuquerque some bracelets with very rich jewels and three jewel boxes of gold. When this ambassador arrived at Malacca, Affonso de Albuquerque had nearly completed the fortress, and placed in it a great quantity of artillery in such order that the ambassador was well pleased. He dismissed the ambassador, giving to him some presents which befitted an ambassador of a King so great . . .

Cronica do Felicissimo Rei D. Manuel
Parte III Capitu. XIX

THE EMBASSY OF MIRANDA DE AZEVEDO TO THE KING OF SIAM (1512) IN COMPANY WITH THE AMBASSADOR OF THE KING OF SIAM AS DESCRIBED BY DAMIAM DE GOES

And with this ambassador Affonso de Albuquerque dispatched Antonio de Miranda de Azevedo and Duarte Coelho as ambassadors to the King, well escorted, through whom he wrote to the King, and sent to him some breastplates of crimson velvet, a helmet, a visor adorned with gold, a suit of armour with white arms, a very splendid oval shield of tapir placed in a sling of brocade, pieces of carved silver with images of animals, and tapestries of gold, and silk, and an animal very well worked with his arsenal.

Cronica do Felicissimo Rei D. Manuel
Parte III Capitu. XIX

THE EMBASSY OF DUARTE COELHO TO THE KING OF SIAM (1516 OR 1518) AS DESCRIBED BY JOAM DE BARROS (CA. 1496-1570)

Having settled the said things, and thus those of supply and the security of the City, arrangements were made to send Duarte Coelho to the King of Siam with letters and a present which the King D. Manuel sent to him in the Armada in which Antonio de Saldanha departed from this Kingdom in 1517. And this in return for what the same King had sent to him by Antonio de Miranda [de Azevedo], when he was sent there by Affonso de Albuquerque as Ambassador, after he captured Malacca, in the company of which went the same Duarte Coelho, as was said previously. Furthermore during the time he was there he came to know well the things of Siam, and in the past year as he was travelling with Fernão Peres de Andrade towards China, he arrived at the coast of the Kingdom of Siam after he encountered a storm, and he entered it by the river Menam which flows through it; on the banks of which is situated the city of Ayudhya, head of the Kingdom, thirty leagues from which he wintered that year, and he returned from there to make his way to China, where he was going, as we said; and from this time he had great intelligence, knowing the things of that place, in which he was well versed: thus for these reasons D. Aleixo [de Menezes] dispatched him in a ship, in which he sent him well escorted. And the substance of his embassy was the confirmation of the peace which Antonio de Miranda and he settled with the King of Siam; and to bring to his attention the benefits which would arise from sending his subjects to settle Malacca, as he now sent to say, because his intention was to expel all the Moors of Malaya from it; and peopling it from his, it would be a means whereby they might better communicate with the Portuguese in amity and peace, and the things of trade would be in his hands, and not in those of the Moors, which had established themselves as the lords of the greater part of the seafaring of all the East. With the said embassy Duarte Coelho departed on July 18th of the year 1518, and he arrived there in November because the ship on which he went was from the Kingdom of Siam and made some stops at the ports along the coast. With the arrival of the embassy the King was well pleased, and he made great honor to him; and when came the time to solemnly swear the things of the peace and friendship, which Duarte Coelho settled with him, in the manner of the sacrament of our religion, he raised a great Cross of wood with the arms of this Kingdom at the foot in a very prominent location in the City, in remembrance and testimony to the peace that he solemnly swore, of which the King was well pleased. And there a few days later at the foot of it, Duarte Coelho buried Pero Lopo, a servant of the Duke of Braganza, D. Jemes, whom he brought with him, as he died of sickness. The King of Siam dispatched Duarte Coelho, very agreeably to the will of the latter, from the city of Ayudhya in November of the year 1519 with three ships, one belonging to him, and two which the same King sent for his protection because of the Armadas of the King of Bintam.

Da Asia de João de Barros
Decada III Livro II Cap. IV

The *Peregrination,* or the embellished chronicle of the adventures of Ferdinand Mendez Pinto (ca. 1510-83)—Portuguese adventurer, wayfarer and soldier of fortune—contains a rare mixture of truth, fantasy and contradiction in a synthesis uniquely entangled. Notwithstanding the *Peregrination* remains an important, virtually the only European source, for the relation of Siamese history during mid-sixteenth century.

Ferdinand Pinto may have been born at Montemor-o-Velho, about the year 1510. He sailed from Portugal for the Orient ca. 1537, and his *Peregrination* contains the narrative of his travels, trade and adventures in virtually every part of Asia. Pinto finally bore his intrepid spirit to Portugal in 1558 and composed his *Peregrination* some time later. His work was published posthumously in 1614.

DESCRIPTION OF THE CIRCUMSTANCES OF THE DEATH OF KING P'RAJAI. KING P'RAJAI DIED IN 1546.

At his arrival [at Ayudhya] the Inhabitants gave him a stately Reception, wherein they bestowed a world of money upon divers Inventions, which were made against his entry. Now whereas during the six moneths of the Kings absence, the Queen his Wife had committed Adultery with a Purveyor of her house, named *Uquumcheniraa,* and that at the Kings return she found her self gone four moneths with childe by him, the fear she was in lest it should be discovered made her, for the saving of her self from the danger that threatened her, resolve to poison the King her Husband, as indeed, without further delaying her pernicious intention, she gave him in a Mess of Milk, which wrought that effect; as he died of it within five days after; during which time he took order by his Testament for the most important affairs of his Kingdom, and discharged himself of the obligation wherein he stood ingaged to the Strangers which had served him in the War of *Chiammay.*

DESCRIPTION OF THE EXCELLENT CHARACTER OF KING P'RAJAI BY PINTO, CONTRARY TO WHAT IS KNOWN FROM SIAMESE HISTORY

... the infortunate King yielded up the Ghost in the presence of the most part of the Lords of his Kingdom, for the which all the people made so great demonstrations of mourning, as every where there was nothing but wailing and weeping. Now forasmuch as this Prince had lived in the reputation of being

147

charitable to the poor, liberall in his benefits and recompences, pitifull and gentle toward every one, and above all incorrupt in doing of justice, and chastising the wicked; his Subjects spake so amply thereof in their lamentations, as if all that they said of it was true; we are to believe, that there was never a better King than he, either amongst these Pagans, or in all the Countries of the world. Howbeit, whereas I cannot assure, that those things which they affirmed in their complaints were true, because I did not see them . . .

A Truer Picture of the Character of King P'rajai Is Seen from an Account of the Fear He Inspired, During Preparations for the Chiengmai Campaign, Shortly Before His Death

Withall he caused Proclamation to be made over all the City, *That all such as were neither old nor lame, and so could not be dispensed with for going to this War, should be ready to march within 12 days at the uttermost, upon pain of being burned alive, with perpetual infamy for themselves, and their descendents, and confiscation of their Estates to the Crown:* To which he added many other such great and dreadfull penalties, as the onely recital of them struck terrour, not onely into them of the Country, but into the very strangers, whom the King would not exempt from this War, of what Nation soever they were, for if they would not serve, they were very expresly enjoyned to depart out of his Kingdom within three days. In the mean time so rigorous an Edict terrified every one in such sort, as they knew not what counsel to take, or what resolution to follow.

The Voyages and Adventures of Ferdinand Mendez Pinto, London, 1692.
Translated by Henry Cogan.

CORRIGENDUM

Siam or the History of the Thais from Earliest Times to 1569 A.D., p. 84, l.14—Read: Chu Hou-tsung (1521-66/7).

ADDENDA

Siam or the History of the Thais from Earliest Times to 1569 A.D.,

Refer p. 69, last paragraph.

The reader may peruse with pleasure and learning the travels of Friar Odoricus (Hakluyt's *Voyages*) and Nicolo de' Conti (Frampton's translation) in the lands bordering Siam during the 14th and 15th centuries respectively. The European intellect had already secured a varied knowledge of Southeast Asia, but a picture of our Siam is yet wanting.

Refer p. 93, fifth paragraph.

A short description of the siege of Ayudhya (The Citie of Sion) is rendered in an English translation of Caesar Frederick's travels in Hakluyt's *Voyages*. The Venetian wrongly ascribes the fall of Ayudhya to the year 1567.

INDEX

149

INDEX

INDEX

INDEX

INDEX

INDEX